The Nurse's Writing Handbook

The Nurse's Writing Handbook

Anita Gandolfo, Ph.D.

Associate Professor
Department of English
West Virginia University
Morgantown, West Virginia

Judy Romano, R.N., M.S.N.

Formerly, Instructor
School of Nursing
West Virginia School of Nursing
Morgantown, West Virginia

 APPLETON-CENTURY-CROFTS/Norwalk, Connecticut

0-8385-6997-8

Notice: The author(s) and publisher of this volume have taken care that the information and recommendations contained herein are accurate and compatible with the standards generally accepted at the time of publication.

Copyright © 1984 by Appleton-Century-Crofts
A Publishing Division of Prentice-Hall, Inc.

84 85 86 87 88 / 10 9 8 7 6 5 4 3 2 1

Prentice-Hall International, Inc., London
Prentice-Hall of Australia, Pty. Ltd., Sydney
Prentice-Hall Canada, Inc.
Prentice-Hall of India Private Limited, New Delhi
Prentice-Hall of Japan, Inc., Tokyo
Prentice-Hall of Southeast Asia (Pte.) Ltd., Singapore
Whitehall Books Ltd., Wellington, New Zealand
Editora Prentice-Hall do Brasil Ltda., Rio de Janeiro

Library of Congress Cataloging in Publication Data

Gandolfo, Anita.
    The nurse's writing handbook.

    Bibliography: p.
    Includes index.
    1. Nursing—Authorship. I. Romano, Judy. II. Title.
[DNLM: 1. Writing—Nursing texts. 2. Communication—
Nursing texts. WY 87 G196n]
RT24.G36   1984   808'.06661   83-22305
ISBN 0-8385-6997-8

PRINTED IN THE UNITED STATES OF AMERICA

To our families . . . who alone provide the unique support that makes such a project possible.

Contents

Preface

The purpose of this handbook is to effect change. The text is designed as a self-contained, comprehensive program in writing instruction which focuses on the writing responsibilities of the professional nurse with the goal of helping nurses improve their writing. Our underlying premise is that writing, like nursing, is a process, and the competent writer is one who understands that process and can employ it with skill and care.

In providing a context for the writing process, we have concentrated on the actual writing experiences of nurses in education and practice. This is a unique handbook that will not only provide instruction in writing for nurses during their years of education, but also can be used throughout their careers to develop and expand their skill in written communication as they assume additional professional responsibilities.

Recognizing the reality of nursing education today, we have developed a handbook to teach writing for any class. It can be used to supplement the nursing program at any level and requires neither class time nor separate instruction. It is designed for self-motivated learners who would like to improve their skill in written communication as well as for instructors who want to provide instruction in writing for their students without taking time from nursing instruction. Ideally, students will use this handbook as a resource in preparing the writing assignments for various nursing classes. We have kept "exercises" to a minimum, offering only enough practice to reinforce the basic principles presented in each chapter. Writing is best learned through meaningful writing experiences, and the regular writing assignments of the nursing curriculum will supply sufficient tasks to complement the instruction offered in this handbook. Similarly, graduate nurses who use this handbook as a resource will find significant practice in their professional writing responsibilities to develop the skill and care in writing taught in this handbook.

This handbook is divided into two sections: PROCESS and PRACTICE. The first four chapters (Process) explain the writing process as analogous to the nursing process and introduce writing as a professional responsibility. In addition to explaining how writing is planned and developed, emphasis is placed on correctness in spelling, punctuation, and usage to stress that correctness is the *minimum* competence required of a professional in any field. The three chapters in the second part (Practice) focus on the types of writing experiences nurses most often encounter classified by setting: clinical writing (assessment, care plans, charts); academic writing (reports, research projects, theses); and professional writing (correspondence, résumés, and writing for publication). Although the arrangement of the chapters is sequential, they are self-contained units and can be read separately as well, depending on the needs of the individual learner.

This is *not* a nursing text. Our aim is to complement, not duplicate, nursing instruction. So although we discuss such topics as assessments, care plans, and incident reports, we do so primarily to develop awareness of the language and style of written communication appropriate to those responsibilities. Throughout this handbook, we have tried to be non-prescriptive, so that the text will complement the specific instruction in form and methodology that is part of individual nursing programs. In discussing planning, for example, we have treated it as a stage in the writing process, explaining many of the cognitive dimensions of planning for the writer. But we have avoided presenting any definitive way to organize written work because we recognize that methods are variable. Though methods of instruction and specific writing requirements may vary from setting to setting, the basic process of writing remains unchanged. It is this process we stress throughout this handbook.

Understanding is the beginning of communication—written as well as oral. Our concern throughout this handbook has been to promote facility in written communication through improved understanding of the process that informs all writing.

Acknowledgments

Our thanks to all the nurses who shared their writing experiences with us—Vicki Conner, Mary Friel, Joan DiPasquale—and to Jane Licht of Appleton-Century-Crofts, who conceived the project and supervised its development.

The
Nurse's
Writing
Handbook

PART I

PROCESS

CHAPTER 1

The Nursing Process and the Writing Process

WHY WRITING?

Today's nurses are professional men and women whose careers will take them into a variety of settings within the health care system where they will be called upon to perform many nonclinical professional tasks. Nurses, like physicians, lawyers, business executives, and teachers, need communication skills commensurate with their status and professional obligations. And writing has become an essential component in the career of the professional nurse. Whether it's a client care plan, a graduate thesis, an application to a funding source for a health care program, a professional resume, or an article for a nursing journal (or a letter to the editor!), writing experiences are integral to nursing practice today.

In the clinical setting written communication is essential for providing quality nursing care. From documentation of information obtained, orders written, care given, and evaluations made, written records are a channel of communication among health care professionals. The importance of effective charting cannot be overemphasized, for this written record not only insures quality care for an individual, but the records can be used as an evaluative tool to improve care. They provide statistics and other data that may be studied to establish a base line of information in other health care situations. So important is the information recorded that a patient's chart is a legal document which can be introduced into a court of law as a record of the type and quality of care given or omitted.

And writing experiences are integral to contemporary nursing education as well. The nursing process is not only analogous to the writing process, the nursing process *uses* the writing process. All students know the frustration of doing an assessment that they feel comfortable with and then being unable to communicate that knowledge in a written form. Students often become impatient with the "writing" part of the nursing process, assuming that it is only an educational tool that will disappear with graduation. It is important to understand that not only is writing an integral part of the nursing process (though the *form* of the writing may change), but that the writing process and the nursing process are complementary. Like nursing, writing is a problem-solving process and a process of discovery. It is not enough to be an educated observer: a professional nurse must be able to *communicate* observations.

Fortunately, it is not necessary to acquire separate skills for every writing task. The writing task is problem oriented, and writing is basically a problem-solving process. Thus, the same basic process informs both nursing and writing. As in nursing, writing skill is best developed through understanding the process. To comprehend the process that underlies all the diverse writing tasks is to acquire a basic "tool" which can effect change. It is a commonplace that the nursing process can be applied in all health care settings. As one basic text explains:

> *The use of the nursing process is not limited to any one time, place, or circumstance. Rather it is a tool that is applicable to a diversity of settings. It is useful in the community and in institutions, with groups and with individuals, in health promotion and teaching and in variations from the well state, with infants and with elderly persons, and in critical care and in long-term care. Through continued and concentrated use of the nursing process, skill and ease are developed in employing the process. (Brill, Kilts; 1980).*

Substitute "writing process" for "nursing process," and you have an effective statement about written communication, especially in the first and last sentences. The professional nurse who learns to employ the writing process "with skill and ease" will find it a most useful "tool that is applicable to a diversity of settings."

WHY PROCESS?

In discussing the writing process, it is important to note that we are describing an activity that for most people is synthesized as a cohesive experience. The person who employs the writing process "with skill and care" will rarely separate the component parts consciously. But to *learn* to write effectively, we must observe the process carefully. As nursing students you learn various clinical techniques through detailed instructions. For example, you might be instructed to "glove" according to these steps:

- Remove packet of gloves from outer wrapper.
- Place packet on a clean, dry, flat surface.
- Open packet as if opening a book.
- Arrange packet so cuff ends of gloves are closest to body.
- Do not touch gloves or inner surface of wrapper.
- Use one hand to glove the other.
- Grasp fold of glove cuff with one hand. Slip other hand into glove taking care not to touch outside of glove.
- Adjust gloves as necessary without touching skin, inner surface of glove, or any other nonsterile surface.
- Hands are kept folded at chest level to prevent contamination until procedure begins.

But soon the actions are synthesized, and you glove automatically and quickly. Only if you had to teach the technique to someone else would you describe the steps separately. Once you have mastered a process, you rarely think of the separate components. But when learning—whether it be learning to take a temperature, give an injection, or put on a gown and gloves—attention is paid to each step of the process. It is the same with learning writing. Good writing is not automatic. It is not some "gift," like having perfect pitch or 20/20 vision. There is, of course, a talent for writing; otherwise there would not be professional writers—people who earn their living through their ability to write well. But at the same time writing is a skill that most people can master in relation to their need. If you have the intelligence and energy to be a nurse, then you have the intelligence and energy to master the necessary writing skills your profession requires.

HOW DOES IT WORK?

As we said, the writing task is problem oriented, and the same process informs both the nursing process and the writing process. The writer **assesses** the subject—either in the collection of data, exploration of the topic, or analysis of the problem; **plans** an effective approach—i.e., decides how to organize the material to best meet the writing goal; **intervenes** where necessary—i.e., revises as needed, either in choosing more precise diction, changing the tone, or reorganizing the material more effectively; and **evaluates** the results—i.e., judges the work's effectiveness, frequently from reader response. A writing text might use terms like *prewriting, outlining, editing, proofreading,* or *revising,* but the important thing to note is that the mental activity—solving a problem—is the same in both processes. The following letter illustrates this point.

Michael Ortega is currently completing his army enlistment. He writes to his parents about his career plans, and this is the letter they receive:

Dear Mom and Dad,

I know you've been concerned about my plans for the future since I will be discharged in two months, and I'm writing with great news. As you know, I've been planning to return to college but have been undecided about a career. You also know how enthusiastic I've been about my work as a medical corpsman for the past two years, so it shouldn't surprise you to learn that I've definitely decided to pursue a career as a health care professional.

I've been accepted in the Nursing Program at West Virginia University. With the college credit I already have, I should receive my B.S.N. in three years. This is an excellent opportunity to enter a field in which I already have some experience—thanks to the army.

This decision may come as a surprise to you since only about 3 percent of professional nurses are male, but when I considered the career possibilities in the health professions, only nursing offered the opportunity to do what I've found most rewarding for the past two years. I want to take care of people and be directly responsible for helping them to wellness. I may be a "minority" nurse, but I'll be a dedicated one. I will be home on the 24th as planned and will tell you more about my plans then.

Your son,

Mike

Michael Ortega's letter illustrates the basic interaction in any writing task. While many people think of writing as an activity involving only one individual and a piece of paper, in actual fact the dynamics of the writing process are triangular (Figure 1-1).

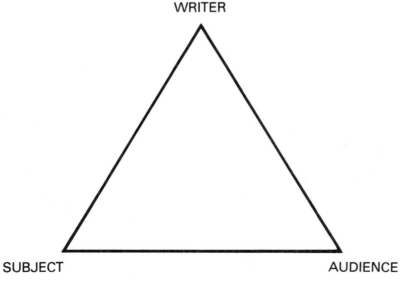

Figure 1-1. The dynamics of the writing process are triangular.

Writing involves a dynamic interaction between writer and audience with due consideraton for subject. In this case, Michael is aware that his parents may be very surprised by his choice of a career in nursing. But he also knows them well and realizes that they are concerned for him and want him to be happy. So he does not tell them in the first sentence, "I've decided to become a nurse," but instead explains that he has had enough experience to know that this is something he really wants to do. He then acknowledges the fact that they may be surprised by his choice but quiets their concern by showing that he has realistically selected this profession.

To highlight the concern for audience in this letter, we might compare the memo that Michael wrote to his supervisor to inform her about his admission to the nursing program.

To: Capt. Carol Berkeley, R.N.

From: Sgt. Michael Ortega, R.N. of the future!

Subject: The future

I received my acceptance from WVU this morning! Hooray! Thanks for all your encouragement and advice.

For a more sympathetic audience—and a person who has been aware of his plans—Sgt. Ortega can announce the news of his acceptance with unrestrained exuberance. All effective writing involves an intent to communicate the subject with a due consideration of audience. As a nurse you will have the advantage of having a clearly defined audience and subject in your professional writing. Your audience will most often be other health professionals (sometimes clients), and your subject will involve client care or other health-related issues. As a professional nurse, you must see yourself as both writer and instructor, conveying vital information to other professionals through writing because it is the most appropriate medium in that particular situation (Figure 1-2).

You enable your audience to become more familiar with, more knowledgeable about, or more aware of the subject through your facility with written communication. Your professional writing responsibilities, whether a nursing care plan, memo, or report, are

NURSE/WRITER

HEALTH CARE   OTHER
                               PROFESSIONALS
                               OR CLIENTS

Figure 1-2. The dynamics of the writing process in nursing.

not onerous tasks that distract you from nursing; they are an integral part of patient care, a reflection of your concern for your clients' well-being.

Michael Ortega may never have seen our "writer's triangle," but he wrote both the letter to his parents and the memo to Capt. Berkeley appropriately. The triangle is only a convenient visual representation of a mental process. This basic dynamic is employed when the writer has a desire to communicate and an awareness of audience. Just as the nurse will care for the client, planning nursing actions for problems identified in the assessment, the writer who is aware of the *process* of writing will select details to best convey the subject to the reader. All good writing focuses on the reader.

Almost a century ago, the novelist Joseph Conrad stated the purpose that lies behind all writing experiences:

My task which I am trying to achieve is, by the power of the written word, to make you hear, to make you feel—it is, before all, to make you see.

Michael Ortega wants his parents to *see* the nursing profession as he does. Similarly, nurses want their readers to *see* their observations. Highly trained observers must be able to transmit what's in the brain to paper. Nursing instructors teach students *what* to observe (assessment), but *how* to transmit those observations effectively requires an understanding of the writing process.

The first step of the writing process has already been completed when the writer gets to the point of wanting to make someone *see*. There is already *content* or *subject* to be expressed. The nurse's subject is always readily identifiable; it's the major impetus to the writing experience. As in the nursing process, the next phase in the writing process is to **plan**—how is the message to be written? Longer writing tasks involve very specific and careful planning, and that will be the subject of Chapter 4. However, all writing takes some planning. The principles to keep in mind are aptly illustrated in Michael Ortega's letter to his parents:

1. **Controlling idea**
2. **Logical order**
3. **Specific details**

These three concepts will apply to any form of written communication, from a charting note to a doctoral dissertation. Note Michael Ortega's controlling idea. There is no doubt what his letter is about, is there? You can't imagine Michael's mother reading the letter and then saying to his father, "I wonder why Mike wrote to us?" or "Mike wrote to say he'd be home soon." The controlling idea pervades the letter, and Michael has chosen specific details to emphasize his main idea. Since he's writing about his choice of career, he doesn't bother telling about the sudden cold spell or the reorganization of his unit at the hospital. All of the information in his letter is subordinate to his controlling idea—"I'm going to be a nurse." And he's chosen a logical order that's best suited to his purpose—and his audience. Since he knows that his parents may be surprised by his choice of a career in nursing, Michael does not begin with the news of his acceptance into the B.S.N. program. Instead, he reminds them of the facts that have contributed to his decision, so that they might be receptive to the news and understand that it is a well-thought-out decision. Knowing his audience and their expectations helped Michael select the appropriate details and present them in a logical order.

It's quite likely that Michael did not sit down and think of the points **controlling idea, specific details,** and **logical order** as he wrote to his parents. Those are terms that writing experts have come up with from observing successful writing and analyzing the reasons for its success. The planning, intervention and evaluation stages in the writing process can be isolated and often are treated separately in lengthy writing projects (like this book!), but in such a short piece of writing as this letter, it's most likely that planning, intervention, and evaluation all occurred simultaneously. If we imagine out hypothetical Michael at work, he sits down and writes a sentence or two, evaluates it for effect, and intervenes as necessary. His thoughts as he writes this letter might have run like this:

Should I tell them right off about nursing school? No, I've never mentioned the possibility to them, and it might be too much of a surprise. I'd better remind them first about the experience I've had as a corpsman and how good it's been. I've already told them a lot about that. I wonder if they'll have any problem with my decision to go for a B.S.N.? They might think I have an unrealistic idea about nursing from being in the service. I'd better put in the fact that I know nursing is only about 3 percent male. I think this is OK—I've emphasized all the things I really think are important, and they should be happy about the fact that it's something I really want to do. I'd better add that we'll talk about it when I come home, so they'll know that I'm open to hearing their views. No. I'd better use the phrase "tell you about." I don't want them to think I'm still undecided and waiting for them to make the decision for me. I want to make sure they know that I'm committed to this. Dedicated! That's a good word. That should do it.

It's clear from Michael's thoughts how the planning, intervention, and evaluation phases of the writing process can work almost simultaneously. That writer's triangle is dynamic, not static. Michael focuses on his purpose, the aim of his writing. He does not see the letter itself as a product, but as a means to an end. So he is constantly evaluating and intervening as needed for the precise effect he wants to achieve.

The successful writer reads what he's written and rescans his writing evaluatively. That might sound obvious, but since we write as we're thinking, studies have shown that most unsuccessful writers do not look at what they've written but simply assume it's what they've *intended* or thought. (That's why writing teachers constantly hear the complaint "But you know what I mean!" from students.) In rescanning, writers simultaneously read and evaluate the effectiveness of their prose and look for the more precise word or phrase or the added detail that will further the overall plan. Such additions (or deletions) are revision. Obviously, in applying this process to a responsibility like charting, it's clear that much of the activity will be done mentally and rapidly, since the chart is a legal document that does not allow for erasure or other revision. We will discuss this further in Chapter 5, "Writing in the Clinical Care Setting." The point is that whether it's a brief note or a 50-page report, the writing experience is based on the same process. And that process must be the basis of the writer's approach to all writing tasks.

In the writing process, as in the nursing process, so much depends upon the attitude of the individual toward his or her role. Nurses who see themselves as hospital drudges would hardly be the most effective care givers, and individuals who see themselves as burdened by writing responsibilities will not be effective writers. For example, let's look at another common situation hypothetically. Three nurses at City Hospital are going to a conference in Washington, D.C., sponsored by the National Institute of Health. Here are the memos they write to their supervisors:

Jan. 19

To: Helen Justiss, R.N.—Head Nurse, OR
From: Betty Johnston

Subject: Schedule

I'm going out of town next month, so please remember that I will be unable to work Feb. 19, 20, or 21.

Jan. 25

To: Mary Dolan, Team Leader—5N
From: David Sullaway
Subject: Scheduling

I will not be available to work Feb. 19, 20, or 21.

Jan. 7

To: Jean Verbosky, Team Leader—18 West
From: Christine Amato
Subject: Days unable to work

Please do not schedule me for work Feb. 19, 20, or 21. I will be in Washington D.C., attending the NIH conference on geriatric nursing. I will be returning on the evening of the 21st and could return to work for 7-3 on Feb. 22.

Writing memos will be covered in more detail in Chapter 7, but the point here is that although the nurse is not *required* to provide the additional information that Christine Amato has included in her memo, such information is relevant and helpful. The writer is clearly thinking of her audience (Jean Verbosky) and includes all information that will be useful to Ms. Verbosky in her professional position. Ms. Amato has *not* included any references to how she's traveling to Washington, where she's staying, what personal shopping she plans to do, or any of the other personal but professionally irrelevant details that might be connected with this trip. As Michael Ortega did in his letter home, Ms. Amato has selected the specific details that pertain to her controlling idea and she has presented them in a logical order.

All writing reflects the writer in some way. The three nurses who wrote memos might be equally competent in patient care, but a supervisor looking at all three memos would form an impression of

Christine Amato as more professionally competent simply because she presents herself so well in her written communication. In the chapters that follow, we will explore the various types of written communication required of the professional nurse and give advice about how to best achieve success in writing. We will consistently emphasize the process as it applies to each type of writing so that the reader will learn to employ the writing process "with skill and care."

All written communication, whether it be a letter to your mother or a memo to your supervisor, employs the writing process. Understanding the process will enable you to develop your ability to communicate effectively in writing. Figure 1-3 illustrates the writing process in relation to the phases of the nursing process. This highlights an important fact about the writing process. Often "writing" is considered the act of putting pen (or typewriter) to paper, but that is only the *third stage* of the process, analogous to "intervention," the action phase of the nursing process. Just as nurses under-

The Nursing Process	The Writing Process
Assessment	Establish *purpose* –identify audience –identify subject –identify writer's role in relation to subject and audience Formulate controlling idea
Plan	Develop supporting statements for controlling idea Arrange supporting statements in logical order
Intervention	Implement the plan with clear, coherent prose that amplifies and illustrates your major ideas
Evaluate	Rescan and revise as needed

Figure 1–3. The same basic problem-solving process informs both writing and nursing.

stand that no plan can be written without a thorough assessment, nurse/writers must realize that the writing process, too, is contingent upon effective "assessment."

WRITING ASSESSMENT

No nurse would give direct patient care without some assessment of the care-giving situation, and no writer should "write" without a preliminary writing assessment. The "writer's triangle" (Figs. 1-1 and 1-2) is a helpful device for a writing assessment. By identifying (even mentally) the audience and subject in relation to the writer's purpose, a controlling idea can be more effectively formulated.

Examples:

Purpose: I am writing to the Director of Nurses to apply for the position of supervisor on the 3-11 PM shift. I have worked at County Hospital for the past five years on this shift and have a total of 11 years nursing experience.

Controlling Idea: I think I am exceptionally qualified for the position of supervisor.

Purpose: I am writing a "nursing practice" paper for my Nursing 341 class. The paper is to be based on some prior clinical experience or volunteer work we have done. I have worked as an aide in pediatrics for two summers and have done a two-month clinical placement in pediatrics.

Controlling Idea: Adequate care for terminally ill children is a goal I would like to achieve as a professional nurse.

Purpose: I am writing a memo to the social worker about Mrs. Battles' nutritional needs. Client

is an 80-year-old diabetic whose disease is
controlled by diet. She lives alone.

Controlling Idea: Mrs. Battles' diet must be regularly and
carefully supervised.

In Chapter 3 we will discuss "planning" in relation to this
initial writing assessment. The "writer's triangle" is basic to all
written communication, and the "blank page" syndrome ("I don't
know how to begin") is most often the result of inattention to this
initial assessment. However, before continuing with a detailed
discussion of the stages of the writing process (Chapters 3 and 4), it
is essential for the writer to consider a personal assessment of
writing strengths and weaknesses with regard to mechanics and
usage. The professional nurse must write with equally professional
competence, and this means that correctness is a *minimum* standard that every nurse must achieve.

EXERCISES

  I. You have been assigned to do a placement at the local Senior
     Center. The staff person in charge is Mildred Jensen, R.N., and
     she has requested a letter from you detailing your experience
     and objectives for this placement.
     A. Write your letter to Ms. Jensen.
     B. Rescan your letter. If you were Ms. Jensen, would you be
        looking forward to meeting the new staff member? Why or
        why not?

 II. You have been offered your "dream job," and you are anxious
     to share the news with your best friend (also an R.N.), your
     nursing advisor, and your widowed mother. Your mother,
     recently disabled in an accident, is currently unable to work
     and is very depressed about her future.
     A. Write the three letters.
     B. Rescan your letters with particular attention to your sense
        of audience.

Do you see evidence of the "writer's triangle" at work? Have you included specific details in a logical order for your particular audience in each separate letter?

III. You have been doing a placement at a convalescent home for the past 6 months, and you will soon be replaced. Since you are well acquainted with your replacement, your supervisor has asked you to write a welcoming letter to the new staff member as a type of informal orientation. Compose the letter by following the phases of the writing process.
1. **Assess** the subject—Explore the topic, collect data, etc. Make notes about what you will write.
2. **Plan** an effective approach—Remember to consider your audience in deciding on the *controlling idea, specific details,* and *logical order.*
3. **Intervene** as needed—Rescan your writing as you are composing the letter, revising where necessary.
4. **Evaluate** the results—After completing the letter, wait a period of time (a few hours to a day) and reread the letter. Return to Phase 3 if necessary.

IV. Write a statement of *purpose* and develop a *controlling idea* for each of the following situations:
A. In your work at the local senior center, you have been asked to write an article for the town's newspaper describing the major needs of the elderly in your area.
B. You have been asked to write a reflection on your experiences as a nursing student for your alumni magazine.
C. The Chamber of Commerce in your town is seeking ways to help the disabled and you decide to make some suggestions based on your experience as a nurse.

REFERENCE

Brill EL, Kilts DF: Foundations for Nursing. New York, Appleton-Century-Crofts, 1980, p 110.

CHAPTER 2

Writing with Skill and Care

WHY CARE?

Correct writing is essential to effective communication. In the last chapter we quoted the writer Joseph Conrad's philosophy of communication, and it is important to repeat it here:

My task which I am trying to achieve is, by the power of the written word, to make you hear, to make you feel—it is, before all, to make you see.

To enable another to *see*, that is, to make visible to another what we ourselves have observed, is the basis of all written communications, whether we are describing the sea in the moonlight or the severity of Mr. Black's chest pains. It is obvious, then, that the medium of this exchange of "vision" must be a set of commonly accepted and understood markers.

There is a powerful scene in the life of Helen Keller that has been beautifully dramatized by William Gibson in *The Miracle Worker* in which the young blind and deaf Helen finally realizes that the letters w-a-t-e-r which her teacher has been patiently spelling into her hand represent a "thing," that liquid she has touched and tasted. This moment unlocks the world of language for her and makes complex communication with others possible for the first time. Helen Keller's experience was dependent on the fact that all English-speaking people understand w-a-t-e-r in the same way. We can sometimes think of "correct" writing as merely the obsession of fussy English teachers, but the world of language which Helen Keller entered that day is dependent upon common agreement about the marks we write on a page—or in a hand.

As Conrad says, the written word has "power," but that power is diminished (or destroyed) by the misuse of the conventions of written language. Every nurse can recognize the importance of the distinction between p.c. and p.o. in an order, yet the layman looking at the two abbreviations may not see much difference. In the same way, the misspelled word, missing comma, or misplaced modifier may not seem important to the inexperienced writer, but there can be serious confusion in communication because of such errors. To write with skill is to have care for another—the reader—and, where client care is the subject of the communication, to have care for the client as well.

Equally important for the professional is the imaging power of the written word. All writing presents the writer as well as the message. Misuse the accepted conventions of written communication, and you present a negative image of yourself. For example, how would you react to reading a statement like this in a nursing journal?

For todays professional nurse communication skills are as important as the technical skills require for practice. Communication is an integral part of the nursing process and the nurse must be proficent in both written and verbal communication.

It is unlikely, of course, that you would find such a seriously flawed piece of writing in any current journal. The statement would have been corrected to read:

For today's professional nurse, communication skills are as important as the technical skills required for practice. Communication is an integral part of the nursing process, and the nurse must be proficient in both written and verbal communication.

In the same way, professional nurses must become competent proofreaders of their own writing. Nurses who "go public" with their writing—whether it be a letter, care plan, or memo—present not only themselves but the nursing profession as well. Since all writing is self-expression, nurses who want to achieve professional status must take the same care to master writing skills that they do to master their clinical skills.

DEVELOPING CARE

Will this book teach you to write correct English prose? No. We can **suggest** how to minimize errors; we can **alert** you to the common errors; we can **show** you how to correct such errors. But make no mistake; the only way to learn to write correctly is to **care** about your writing. You have probably had much instruction in correct usage at various levels of your education. Most, if not all, of the information in this chapter exists somewhere in your consciousness ready to be retrieved. In order to acquire professional competence in writing, you first have to decide that the ability to write correctly is worth your time and attention. For, like all growth, improving your writing skills requires motivation, determination, and effort.

The *only* way to improve your ability to write standard English prose correctly is to become aware of the particular errors that you make. Practicing sample sentences in a writing exercise book is not especially helpful; it is *your own* written discourse that you must learn to correct. Few of us make exactly the same errors or have the identical weaknesses in writing. Your first task is to learn to assess your own writing skills.

To test your present awareness of standard English usage, read the following passage for *correctness,* and take note of each error you find:

Student nurses do not have a common base of current experience with staff nurses in the clinical setting. The student and the staff nurse are at different stage's of development in the nursing system. Both in terms of experience and professionalization. These differences in stage's of development can lead to communication problems. In addition the differences in stages of development also influences how each group perceives the other. The perception of the other group is influenced by a variety of factors that can be catagorized as being either internal (to the individual) or external (to the setting).

Reading over your writing solely to identify errors in the mechanics of writing is a form of *assessment,* and the writing process, like the nursing process, requires regular assessment. You must strengthen your ability to identify problems in your writing so that you can plan the necessary intervention. Test your awareness with the "corrected" version of the passage. How many did you identify in your first reading, and could you "explain" the error?

Student nurses do not have a common base of current experience with staff nurses in the clinical setting. The student and the staff nurse are at different <u>stages</u> of development in the

1

nursing <u>system, both</u> in terms of experience and professionali-

2

zation. These differences in <u>stages</u> of development can lead to

3

communication problems. In addi<u>tion,</u> the differences in <u>stages</u>

4   3

of development also <u>influence</u> how each group perceives the

5

other. The perception of the other group is influenced by a variety of factors that can be <u>categorized</u> as being either inter-

6

nal (to the individual) or external (to the setting).

How well did you do?

1. ***Plural versus possessive.***   The confusion between plural and possessive is very common and yet is an easy prob-

lem to correct. If you do not yet know when, why, and how to use the apostrophe, you need to spend some time with that marker right now in your writing career.

2. *Sentence fragment.* This is something the nurse must be particularly aware of since fragments are the basis of charting, yet they are grammatically incorrect and should be avoided in all other written communication. The nurse must perfect the technique of writing effective fragments in charting (see Chapter 5) but also understand sentence structure enough to avoid the fragment in other writing.

3. Do you understand the *apostrophe* yet?

4. *Use of the comma.* This particular use of the comma (after an introductory phrase) usually presents no problem for most writers. But do you know the other times when a comma must be used?

5. *Subject/verb agreement.* A real example of how important care is in writing; subject and verb must agree in number, but when the subject is divided from its verb by a phrase we sometimes forget to recheck to see if we're making the right words agree. It is natural to link the verb to the closest noun—the words we "hear" together as we read. It is "differences/influence" not "development/influences."

6. *Spelling.* As in this sample, many spelling problems are caused by an attempt to spell words as they're said rather than as they're written. Beware of the fallacy of phonetic spelling; only in charades is what "it sounds like" important.

Remember, though, that rescanning someone else's prose is a poor substitute for rescanning your own writing. Being aware of your friend's weakness for chocolate chip cookies will not help you lose ten pounds. A good way to practice writing with care is to compose about a page on any topic you wish, concentrating on writing as correctly as you are able. Wait at least three hours before you attempt an assessment. Then you should carefully rescan the paper—just for *correctness,* circling any errors you find. Next, plan your intervention; i.e., decide how you will revise for accuracy. Some errors can be corrected in only one way (spelling errors, for example), but others offer choices. To be able to rescan your writing effectively and make proper revisions, you should be familiar with the material in the survey of skills on the following pages. When you are faced with doubt in writing ("to apostrophe or not to apostrophe—that is the question"), unless you know the *rationale* for the choice you make, you just perpetuate the doubt. To understand the choice is to gain control of your writing and be able to use it as an effective professional tool.

BUILDING SKILLS

Note that although conventional labels are used here for convenience and clarity, it is not important that you be able to identify the error by "name" e.g., sentence fragment, comma splice. The skill you are developing is the ability to assess the correctness of your writing and to intervene as necessary.

Punctuation

Before discussing the comma, semicolon, and other "mysterious" symbols, we must address two common errors that are corrected with punctuation but are actually mistakes in sentence construction. They plague most inexperienced writers and reflect a lack of control of language.

> Nursing is a highly diverse profession there are opportunities for the generalist as well as the specialist.

or

> Nursing is a highly diverse profession, there are opportunities for the generalist as well as the specialist.

Neither sentence is correct.

The first sentence would be called "run on" and the second "comma splice." This is a very common pattern in writing and is understandable—but is *always incorrect*. Such sentences result from the rapid flow of ideas related in thought. The basic rule to remember is that *when two separate sentences are joined, there must be some definite connective, and the comma alone is never sufficient.*

In planning and intervention, the writer has several possible options:

Option 1. Nursing is a highly diverse profession. There are opportunities for the generalist as well as the specialist.

   Writer separates the two complete sentences.

Option 2. Nursing is a highly diverse profession; there are opportunites for the generalist as well as the specialist.

   Writer strengthens the internal punctuation; a semicolon can join two complete sentences.

Option 3. Nursing is a highly diverse profession, for there are opportunities for the generalist as well as the specialist.

   Writer adds a coordinating conjunction (and, but, or, so, for, nor, yet). Note that the comma is retained before the conjunction.

Option 4. Nursing is a highly diverse profession with opportunities for the generalist as well as the specialist.

   Writer subordinates one word group to combine the two sentences into one.

Remember that the choice of intervention is up to the writer. That is, all four examples are "correct", so the writer will choose the form that best fits his or her context and style.

Fragment
Another common sentence error is the *fragment,* which, as its label implies, might be thought of as a "piece" of a sentence. Most often it is a subordinate clause that has gotten separated from its main clause. That is, a fragment is a portion of thought that cannot stand on its own *grammatically.*

Nurses are very familiar with sentence fragments because that is the form in which most charting is done. On the patient's chart, information must be communicated as succinctly as possible without losing meaning. So the complete grammatical unit:

The patient complained of substunal chest pain radiating into the left jaw and left arm.

will be charted:

c/o substunal chest pain radiating into (L) jaw and (L) arm

Other than the abbreviations, what is the major difference in the charting note? It eliminates "the patient"—the subject of the sentence—since that notation would be superfluous on the patient's chart. A sentence without a subject, however is *grammatically* incorrect, and, aside from recording, should be avoided.

The sentence fragment is usually a result of improperly dividing thought units. For example, you can probably guess that these "sentences" are incorrect:

1. Besides improving patient knowledge.
2. To develop a meal plan using the exchange system.
3. Such as increasing breast size and muscle mass.

Do they seem more correct written this way?

1. Besides improving patient knowledge. Patient education can reduce the length of hospital stays and readmission rates.
2. To develop a meal plan using the exchange system. The following steps must be taken for each patient.
3. The oral contraceptive pill has some side effects. Such as increasing breast size and muscle mass.

These examples are, of course, equally incorrect. The point is that fragments rarely exist in isolation—except when deliberately written on a chart. The fragment is a portion of thought that is logically connected to another thought in the writer's mind but cannot be separated grammatically. Each of these "sentences" is one sentence consisting of a main clause and a subordinate clause. The latter, as its name indicates, cannot be separated—as the first group of "sentences" above illustrates. Correctly written, the sentences would be:

1. Besides improving patient knowledge, patient education can reduce the length of hospital stays and readmission rates.
2. To develop a meal plan using the exchange system, the following steps must be taken for each patient.
3. The oral contraceptive pill has side effects, such as increasing breast size and muscle mass.

Fragments are easy to spot in rescanning *with care*. If you rescan by reading thought units, you are likely to make the same mistake as when you wrote the sentences incorrectly. You *read* them as one unit; they are *written* as two. You must deliberately read from period to period, making sure that each separate sentence can exist as an independent unit. Some advice: if you have difficulty forgetting the "thought," while you're reading, try rescanning your writing from *end to beginning*. Start with the last sentence; check that; go on to the next-to-last sentence, etc. Especially if fragments are a problem for you. (Oops!)

Punctuation Pointers

Comma.   The comma signals a minor pause in the sentence, but you don't simply insert a comma wherever you *sense* such a pause. There are specific *grammatical* pauses which dictate the use of the comma, and writers must be familiar with those situations and use the comma accordingly.(Can you explain our use of the comma so far in this paragraph?) The rules governing the use of the comma are easy to understand, and only one situation actually gives writers any trouble. To review: Use a comma

Between Items In A Series

High pay, flexible schedules, and good benefits make City Hospital an ideal place to work.

Most writers have little difficulty here.

Note, however:

The comma before the conjunction is optional but often used to prevent ambiguity. For example, both of the following sentences are technically correct:

1. Geneticists, gynecologists, and sex counselors are available in many locations.
2. Geneticists, gynecologists and sex counselors are available in many locations.

In this case, the subjects are three separate groups of professionals, but the omission of the comma in Sentence 2 might suggest (especially to an uninformed reader) that there are only two groups, i.e., that some professionals are both gynecologists and sex counselors. To avoid such possible confusion, you should use the final comma before the conjunction.

To Set Off Introductory Material

1. Because it was their first day on the unit, the students spent more time with each patient.
2. Balancing himself carefully, Jim finally tried walking with his crutches.

Usually we are aware of the strong grammatical pause in such sentences (even if we don't know the "label"), and this use of the comma is rarely violated. One problem occurs when the introductory element is especially long:

3. Whenever I get up really early in the morning and have time to read the paper and relax with a second cup of coffee, I find I have a better day.

The problem here is not so much forgetting the comma as forgetting the opening "Whenever" that subordinates the first clause. Writers often unthinkingly use a period after such a long grammatical unit and wind up with a sentence fragment.

When the introductory element is very short, the comma can be omitted.

4. In my opinion Jack is tops!

But the writer must always be alert to the danger of ambiguity in such situations.

5. When the chaplain entered the waiting room became silent.

A comma after "entered" is indicated here in spite of the short introductory element to caution the reader not to read the first phrase incorrectly. "When the chaplain entered the waiting room . . . ." The purpose of punctuation is to facilitate, not confuse, reading. Since it is *never incorrect* to use a comma after the introductory element, it is a good practice to always use one unless you have very definite reasons for the omission.

To Set Off Parenthetical Elements *(words or phrases that interrupt the flow of thought in a sentence)*

1. My sister Helen, the family brain, has a Ph.D. in biochemistry.
2. Steve Yura is a very reliable orderly, in my opinion.

This situation usually poses no problem for writers. Even if they don't know the technical reason for the comma, most writers are sensitive to the grammatical separation of parenthetical elements and punctuate accordingly.

ONE CAUTION:

Compare these two sentences:

1. Wilma Davis, who lives next door, is a nurse-epidemiologist.
2. The woman who lives next door is a nurse-epidemiologist.

Both sentences are punctuated correctly. Why the difference in the use of the comma? The first sentence tells us that Wilma Davis is a noted nurse-epidemiologist, and the information that she "lives next door" is extra, not essential to the meaning of the sentence. In Sentence 2, however, you are not saying that "The woman is a nurse-epidemiologist"; your reader would ask "Which woman?" So the information, "who lives next door," is *essential* to the sentence (in helping to identify the subject; not "The woman" but "The woman who lives next door") and therefore is *not* set off by commas.

Another example:

1. Children, who are ill, require sympathy and understanding.
2. Children who are ill require sympathy and understanding.

Which is the correct sentence?

Obviously we might argue that *all* children require sympathy and understanding, but the way Sentence 1 is punctuated *all children are ill!* Clearly the writer intends to talk about "children who are ill" and what the requirements are in caring for them, so Sentence 2 correctly reflects that meaning.

Similarly:

1. Adults who are diabetic require a carefully controlled diet.

but

2. Mr. Mason, who is a diabetic, finds shift work difficult.

Can you understand this distinction? It is not all adults who require a carefully controlled diet but "adults who are diabetic." The entire phrase functions as the subject of the sentence and should not be separated by punctuation. But in Sentence 2 it is Mr. Mason who finds shift work difficult, and the fact that he is diabetic is offered as an explanation for his difficulty and is not grammatically essential to the sentence. Thus, it is correctly set off by commas.

To Connect Two Complete Sentences Joined by a Coordinating Conjunction (and, but, for, or, nor, so, yet)

Remember our compound sentence:

Nursing is a highly diverse profession, for there are opportunities for the generalist as well as the specialist.

This is the use of the comma that is most often misunderstood. It is not the conjunction that requires the comma but the joining of two complete sentences with a conjunction. If you are merely joining separate items with a conjunction, there is no comma.

Medications may be prepared in a medication room $\underset{1}{\underline{and}}$ dis-

tributed via a tray $\underset{2}{\underline{or}}$ cart $\underset{3}{\underline{or}}$ prepared directly from a rolling

cart which is taken to the bedside.

Three conjunctions and no commas!

1. "prepared" *and* "distributed"—conjunction links two verbs
2. "tray *or* cart"—conjunction links two nouns
3. "prepared and distributed" *or* "prepared directly"—conjunction links the double predicate of the sentence

But note the comma now:

Medications may be prepared in a medication room and distributed via a tray or cart, or they may be prepared directly from a rolling cart which is taken to the bedside.

By adding "they" to the second predicate, we have formed a second complete sentence, so the conjunction is now preceded by a comma.

Rather than determine whether or not the conjunction requires a comma (i.e., *write with care*), many writers simply add a comma before every coordinating conjunction BUT *superfluous commas are as incorrect as missing commas!*

Note the difference:

1. That essay has mature style and vivid use of language.

2. That essay has mature style, and the writer uses language vividly.

Unless you understand why both of these sentences are punctuated correctly, you will not be able to use commas confidently.

If you are undecided about using a comma, check your sentence with the situations discussed in this section. A good rule of thumb is *that if you can't* find a reason for the comma and the sentence is not confusing without it, omit the comma.

Semicolon.   The main use of the semicolon is to mark the separation of two complete thoughts (see Option 2, p. 25):

> Nursing is a highly diverse profession; there are opportunities for the generalist as well as the specialist.

The tendency of many writers is to use a comma here instead of a semicolon, thereby creating the grievous error known as the comma splice. The comma splice connotes ignorance and/or laziness and indifference, none of which are qualities that enhance the image of the professional nurse.

The semicolon is also used to mark off items in a series when the items themselves contain commas.

> **Example:**   The home health care program is affiliated with Mercy Hospital, Welch; Preston Memorial Hospital, Kingwood; and Valley Community Hospital, Weirton.

Colon.   The colon is a mark of punctuation that introduces information. Use the colon at the end of a complete statement to introduce a list, a long quotation, or an explanation.

Examples:

1. Kübler-Ross has identified five stages in the grieving process: denial, anger, bargaining, depression, and acceptance.
2. Kübler-Ross has some interesting comments on the fear of death:

It is inconceivable for our unconscious to imagine an actual ending of our own life here on earth, and if this life of ours has to end, the ending is always attributed to a malicious intervention from the outside by someone else. In simple terms, in our unconscious mind we can only be killed; it is inconceivable to die of a natural cause or of old age. Therefore death in itself is associated with a bad act, a frightening happening, something that in itself calls for retribution and punishment.

(From *On Death and Dying,* 1970)

3. To all this information about punctuation, I would add a final point: common sense is essential.

Dash.   The dash is used like the colon in Example 3. The only real distinction is that the dash is used more "dashingly"—and less frequently. That is, the dash most often sets off words for dramatic effect and should be used sparingly.

Example:

1. It's not as bad as you think—it's worse.
2. I have no problems with my supervisor because I know exactly what she expects—total perfection at all times.
3. Life is just a bowl of cherries—pits and all.

The dash adds flavor to your writing and might really be considered more an aspect of style rather than mechanics. Like most "flavorings," it should be used with restraint; do not let it become an affectation in your writing.

Note: *The dash is formed on the typewriter by striking the hyphen twice with no spacing before or after (--).*

The dash is especially helpful in writing effective clinical nursing notes (see Chapter 5).

Hyphen.   Only one use of the hyphen regularly causes difficulty for writers. *The hyphen is used to connect two adjectives that precede a noun and function as one word in describing that noun.*

Examples:

1. Well-child care is an important area of pediatric nursing.
2. Alertness is important in dealing with life-threatening situations.

CAUTION:

The compound adjective should not be confused with the adverb-adjective-noun construction which is *not* hyphenated.

Example: That was a poorly written exam.

Although both modifiers are needed for the full meaning of the sentence, the "ly" is a clue that the adverb is at work, and there is no hyphen.

Examples: 1. The patient had a slightly elevated temperature.
2. He was a neatly dressed gentleman.

Agreement

Agreement is a comparatively simple concept, but it requires *care* in writing. Errors in agreement are common and indicate slovenly writing, a poor image for the professional nurse.

Subject-Verb Agreement

The verb of a sentence agrees in number with its subject. That is, if your subject is singular, the verb is singular as well (The boy is tall). A plural subject requires a plural verb (The boys are tall).

Problems arise when the writer has difficulty identifying subject and verb.

1. People, regardless of their nationality, race, or social class, are often irrational.
2. The decisions of the therapist seem questionable.

When other words intervene between the subject and verb, you must be careful in making the proper agreement. In these sentences the agreement is correct between *people/are* and *decisions/seem.*

Another confusing situation is when the verb comes before the subject. In English sentences, the subject usually comes before the verb. When sentences are inverted (verb before subject), the writer has to be sure to make the right words agree.

Example: In the small tent, there were 16 frightened children.

Were is plural because the subject is plural. Children *is the subject even though it is the last word in the sentence.*

Example: There are many ways to skin a cat.
No, cat *is not the subject.* Are *is plural to agree with the subject* ways.

This may be confusing when we are dealing with practice senten-ces, but remember, you are going to practice correcting *your own* writing, so the "subject" should be clear to you since it is what you are writing about.

Pronoun Agreement.   Since pronouns are words that take the place of nouns (as you learned way back in elementary school), every pronoun is related to the noun it has replaced. That noun is known as the pronoun's *antecedent.* In the sentence

The patient could not find his room.

the antecedent of *his* is clearly *patient.* Because the two words are interchangeable, they agree in number, and the singular patient is replaced by a singular pronoun. (If the patient were female the pronoun would be *her,* of course.) The indefinite pronouns— another, anybody, anyone, anything, each, either, everybody, every-one, everything, neither, no one, nobody, nothing, one, somebody, someone, something—*all take singular pronouns.* The problem here is with *everybody* and *everyone.* Many writers tend to think logically but not grammatically. That is, according to the sense of the sentence, *everybody* might mean a lot of people, so it is assigned a plural pronoun.

Everybody has to do their own work.

This is incorrect. Regardless of the number of people involved, grammatically "everybody" is singular. (Note that the verb is singular. A good practice when in doubt about the pronoun for an indefinite pronoun subject is to check your verb.)

Another reason for the tendency to use plural pronouns for indefinite pronoun antecedents is the attempt to avoid sexism or awkwardness.

Everybody has to do his or her own work.

This is correct but awkward. While it is never incorrect to use the masculine form alone (his own work), there is the taint of sexist language that writers are more conscious of today.When dealing with your own writing, it is often possible to avoid this problem by switching to a plural subject:

All people have to do their own work.

Misplaced Modifiers
This is a topic that usually provides a few chuckles because the careless position of modifiers in a sentence can present some really ludicrous situations.

The Grants adopted a baby from a home with blond curls and dimples.

Most readers would mentally adjust to the fact that it's the baby and not the home that has the curls and dimples. However, misplaced modifiers are a serious consideration for the nurse whose writing must be as precise as possible, particularly in the clinical setting. It is not the error in itself that is a problem for the nurse, but the possibility of ambiguity in written orders and the indication of sloppy thinking that such structures reflect.

The patient complained of leg cramps on Friday.

Did the patient have the leg cramps on Friday or report them on Friday? Perhaps both, but the sentence is ambiguous as written.

Rule: *Place words as close as possible to what they describe.*

Clearer: On Friday, the patient complained of leg cramps.

Dangling Modifiers

More confusing are modifiers without a word to modify!

Having closed the doors, sleep was possible.

Who closed the doors? Obviously not "sleep," so we know that there's some error here. But what about this revised sentence?

Having closed the doors, the patient was able to sleep.

This *could* be correct if the patient had closed the doors. But what if the writer was actually trying to explain that the aide closed the doors? The sentence should read:

After the aide closed the doors, the patient was able to sleep.

As we advised at the beginning of this chapter, rescanning will take care of most of the careless errors in writing. Both dangling and misplaced modifiers will become apparent if you rescan *with care.* Make sure that what you plan to say is not only in your head but actually on the paper as well.

Apostrophe

The apostrophe is interesting because one of its uses gives hardly any trouble at all, and the other is a constant problem.

Most writers have mastered the apostrophe in contractions. *Can't, won't, you're* are usually written correctly except when *you're* is *carelessly* written as *your.*

However, when the apostrophe is used to show possession, chaos reigns. Many writers are so unsure of the plural and/or possessive forms that they tend to "play it safe" by omitting the apostrophe entirely. The only way to solve the dilemma is to get the differences straight in your mind, and then pay *careful attention* to the use of the apostrophe in all your writing until you use the possessive forms appropriately and with confidence.

Example: the client's rights
the operation's success
anybody's opinion

No problem so far, is there? The apostrophe plus *s* (if the word does not end in *s*) is the easiest way to show possession in English.

Note: Though we might not commonly think of an "operation" possessing anything, if we rephrase to "the success of the operation," we can see the necessity for considering the possessive—i.e., success is a property of the operation.

For plural words ending in *s* or *z* sound, only an apostrophe is added.

Example: the workers' strike
my parents' home
But: the children's toys

Children is plural but does not end in *s*, so the possessive is made by the apostrophe + *s*.

Example: the women's club
the men's store

One area of confusion is singular words that end in an *s* or *z* sound. For example, how would you write:

the cat of Mr. Jones
the desk of my boss
the law of Moses
the debut of the actress

Like this:

> Mr. Jones's cat
> my boss's desk
> Moses' law
> the actress' debut

> **Rule:** *Singular words ending in s or z sound; add apostrophe +s for words of one syllable. Add only the apostrophe for words of more than one syllable.*

How will you keep that straight? Learn it. It's the only way. (It is helpful to keep two examples in your head, e.g., Jones's and Moses'.)

Note: Pronouns that show possession *never* take an apostrophe—so it's *his, hers, its, ours, yours, theirs, whose.*

> *Remember that "it's" is always "it is."*

> *It's* a boy!
> The midnight shift rapidly lost *its* appeal.

> *Remember* that simple plurals never take an apostrophe.

> *You may write:* We went to ladies' night.
> Never *write:* They had a special night for ladies'.

For some reason, words ending in s seem to evoke an apostrophe from writers who perhaps feel "when in doubt, add an apostrophe" (probably the same people who are addicted to superflous commas).

If you know that you are not sure of yourself in using the apostrophe, don't try to memorize all this. Simply think twice whenever you find yourself using the apostrophe, and consult these pages whenever necessary. Correctness is the result of *care.*

Spelling

Correct spelling is more a matter of knowledge than intelligence. If you misspell a word, you simply do not know how it should be spelled—but *you can learn.* All of us have some words that we can't spell or are unsure of; some people have more doubtful words than others. But the knowledge to acquire is not how to spell every word in the English language; it is to become aware of your particular spelling weaknesses so you can strengthen them.

For nurses, spelling is particularly important. They can't afford to be careless because so many of the words they must use daily as part of the specialized vocabulary of health care are difficult to spell, and misspelling them projects an unprofessional image. Consider the nurse who would write

pupils were *dialated*	*for*	pupils were *dilated*
cathata removed	*for*	*catheter* removed
abdamen firm	*for*	*abdomen* firm

Such poor spelling would reflect negatively on a nurse, and most nurses have mastered the specialized health care vocabulary through education and practice. Yet the nurse who often has mastered such technical and difficult words as *menorrhagia, exudate, neuralgia,* and *oophorectomy* must also be careful not to be writing *thier, ocassion,* or *writting*—common spelling errors among the general population. Every time a nurse writes publicly, whether it be a care plan, memo, or business letter, that communication is a professional responsibility and should reflect competence in both technical and ordinary usage.

IMPROVING YOUR SPELLING

In the Appendix to this book, you will find a list of "spelling demons," words commonly misspelled in all forms of written communication. You might test yourself to determine your overall spelling competence. If you find (or are already aware) that you have problems with spelling, there are some specific steps you can take to improve your spelling.

1. Avoid phonetic spelling when you're unsure of a word. Most often this results in such errors as *definately* for *definitely* and *seperate* for *separate.* To "spell it the way it sounds" is always a risky business in the English language because our language is so phonetically idiosyncratic. If you have to rely on "sounding it out," that's the cue to head for the dictionary.

2. Learn to rely on the dictionary. The common complaint is "How can I use the dictionary when I can't spell the word?" Easy— explore the alternatives. That's not difficult when it's the ending of the word you are unsure of:

accidently *or* accidentally????

You simply look up *accident*, and you will find *accidentally* right away. But this method is not impossible when it's the first part of the word you're not sure of. Suppose you're not sure how to spell the word *illicit*. By the sound of it, it could be *alisit; elicit;* or *illicit*— depending on your pronunciation. But you know from the sound that the word will begin either *al, el,* or *il.* (This is one time when it's all right to work phonetically!) Check each of them until you find your word. One problem may be that if you work systematically you would find *elicit* first, but since you're working with *care,* you'll check the definition and realize that's not the word you have in mind, and at least one pair of "words commonly confused" (see next section in this chapter) will no longer be confusing. By using the dictionary, the process of exploring for the correct spelling can become a real learning experience.

3. Keep a list of words you're unsure of. Most of us have a few words that we just can't keep straight and don't use frequently enough to master. It's helpful to keep a personal spelling list for these words for easy reference. Some people keep such a list in their dictionary or in a desk drawer that's handy. You will find it easier to consult this list every time the word comes up (rather than thumbing through the dictionary), and in the process of regularly consulting the list you'll find that you eventually master the word. Figure 2-1 shows such a personal spelling list. Adding personal notes about your difficulty with the word often helps mastery. It's best to master spelling demons as part of the process of writing rather than trying to memorize lists of words.

4. Recall spelling rules. In spite of the fact that from the first

Enter here the words you misspell in your writing tasks. If you add to and study this list regularly, you will learn to visualize the word written correctly and not repeat the errors.

Correct Spelling	Notes to Remember

Figure 2-1. Personal spelling assessment.

grade we're taught to chant *"i before e except after c or when sounded as a,"* many people continue to write *recieve* for *receive* and *beleive* for *believe*. If you know such spelling rules, it's helpful to recall them when you are trying to spell particular words. Figure 2-2 illustrates four common spelling rules which are helpful to learn.

5. Be aware of spelling patterns. There are certain words that many people have difficulty spelling because of the basic pattern, whether it's words ending in "ing,' or "ence" versus "ance," or homonyms, etc. Listed below are commonly misspelled words by

RULE 1:	*i* before *e* except after *c* or when sounded like *a*
	So: field, yield *But:* receive, conceive *and* eight, weight
	Common Exceptions: either leisure foreign science

RULE 2:	Words that end in *y* and have a consonant before the *y*, change the *y* to *i* before adding a suffix
	So: fly = flies carry = carried
	But NOT if the suffix begins with *i* (as in *"ing"*):
	study+ing = and try+ing = trying
	Common Exceptions: lay to laid, say to said, pay to paid

RULE 3:	Words ending in silent *e* usually drop the *e* before a suffix beginning with a vowel and retain the *e* if the suffix begins with a consonant
	So: use becomes using and useless
	Common Exceptions: argument judgment truly noticeably changeable courageous canoeing mileage
	(Note how many of these "exceptions" are spelling demons!)

RULE 4:	When you add a suffix to a word that ends in a consonant, the consonant is doubled if:
	1. the suffix begins with a vowel:
	clot becomes clotting
	2. the word is one syllable or is accented on the last syllable:
	admit becomes admitting *But* visit becomes visiting

Figure 2-2. Four helpful spelling rules.

pattern. Check yourself to see how many you can readily spell and how many you should add to your personal spelling list.

I. The difference between *ance* and *ence* is frequently difficult to "hear." If you have a problem in this area, many of these words may have to be memorized correctly. If you rely on guessing, you may be wrong 50 percent of the time!

abundance	performance
acceptance	existence
attendance	independence
acquaintance	presence
appearance	convenience
significance	experience
admittance	intelligence
guidance	audience
ignorance	difference

II. Doubled consonants are always a problem because we often "hear" only one sound. These frequently used words should be memorized:

accommodate	parallel
apparent	preferred
exaggerate	accidentally
unnecessary	committee
embarrass	transferred
occurred	

III. Beware of words that are frequently misspelled with a double consonant where there should be only one!

commitment . . . . *only one t*
tenant . . . . *only one n*
writing . . . *only one t* (possibly confused because of *written*)
benefited . . . . *only one t*

IV. There is often confusion about whether or not to drop the final *e* before adding a suffix. In spite of the rule (or perhaps because there are so many exceptions to the rule), this is difficult to master. Be familiar with these regularly used words:

Drop final e	**Keep final e**
hoping	sincerely
becoming	management
truly	noticeable
argument	arrangement
judgment	
losing (There is a tendency not only to write *loseing* but also *loosing.*)	
excitable	

V. In spite of warnings about the dangers of phonetic spelling, some words in our language are regularly misspelled because of their confusing "sound." Note the following:

category	*often misspelled as* catagory
environment	*the* ironm *combination has to be said very carefully to hear all the sounds*
familiar ⎱ peculiar ⎰	*you don't hear the* liar *in these words*
rhythm	*a word that almost* has *to be memorized—the sounds are so confusing*
article	cle *sounds like* cal
condemn	*remember that final* n
fascinating	sc *says* s *here*
guaranteed	ua *sounds like* a
knowledge ⎱ privilege ⎰	*note which one has the* ledge

schedule	*remember the* h
tragedy	*commonly misspelled as* tradgedy
conscious	*what the alert patient is*
conscience	*what tells you right from wrong*
conscientious	*a quality of being responsible and reliable*
prejudice	*a noun—note that the verb is* prejudiced
disastrous	*remember to leave the final e out of* disaster

WORDS COMMONLY CONFUSED

Nurses familiar with the language of recording will recognize that the following pairs of common abbreviations may *appear* similar but have significantly different meanings:

B.M.	I.U.P.
B.P.	I.V.P.
U.R.I.	T.U.R.
U.T.I.	T.P.R.

Part of your clinical training is to recognize such abbreviations and use them appropriately. You would feel extremely embarrassed confusing B.M. for B.P.

Nurses are usually quite careful of their "technical" language, but as *professionals* they must become equally aware of the words of ordinary English usage that are commonly confused and used incorrectly. Just as your charting should be precise, accurate, and clear, so the letters, memos, and reports you write should reflect a similar control of language.

Words that are commonly confused are listed in every English handbook, but only you can eliminate the problem in your own writing. What are the words you misuse? The following list includes some of the most frequently confused words; how many do you recognize as problems for you? (These are just a few of the most common problems in word usage. If the word you are looking for is not here, consult any good college dictionary.)

a lot–two words, often misspelled as *alot*. That is always incorrect, but somehow large numbers of people have adopted this nonstandard usage. Don't be one of them!

all right–never *alright*; always two words

then, than–*than* is used mainly in comparisons; greater *than*, less *than*, more important *than*, etc.

–*then* denotes sequence: *then* I will go; *then* comes growth; *then* ice the cake

affect, effect–*affect* is principally used as a verb; *effect* as a noun

How did Arizona affect your asthma?
What were the effects of living in Arizona?

–but *effect* is sometimes a verb

Did living in Arizona effect a change in your health?

accept, except–*accept* means to receive

He accepted the invitation to speak.

–*except* always refers to exclusion

All passed, except George Thompson.
Dr. Smith excepted Greg Lewis from the exam.

allusion, illusion–*allude* means to refer to something indirectly; *illusion* is an unreal image or false impression

We knew that the mention of alcohol was an allusion to our late-night escapades.
He lived with the illusion that he would recover, but the doctors had little hope.

could of, should of–*could have; should have* (writer hears the contraction *could've* or *should've* and creates this error)

fewer, less–*fewer* refers especially to number; *less* refers to value, degree, or amount

Fewer than twenty students passed.
There is less chance of failure with study.

irregardless–*always* incorrect; the word is *regardless*

lose, loose–*loose* is what your shoelaces become; *lose* is what you do with a bet or what happens to your marbles

used to, supposed to–don't forget the final -*d*; common error is *use to* or *suppose to*

> *He used to be an important man around here.*
> *Aren't you supposed to be on duty now?*

EXERCISES FOR FURTHER ASSESSMENT*

I. *Supply capitalization and punctuation as needed:*
Gerontology is a rapidly expanding speciality among health care and social service professions research in the problems of the elderly in society has led to an awareness of the stereotypes with which many americans approach the aged and a reexamination of our traditional ways of treating older people old age usually considered that period from age 65 on is a somewhat arbitrary designation depending on an individuals ability to adapt to the inevitable physical loss a loss which varies from person to person the contemporary gerontologist must have a knowledge of the physical and psychological needs of the individual and above all be a caring professional interested in each clients well being.

II. *Supply internal punctuation as needed:*
1. The students will be responsible for medications, vital signs and treatments.
2. With the advent of the pediatric nurse practitioner well child care has undergone some significant changes.
3. Nurses who work in the Emergency Department are able to handle stressful situations.
4. Mrs. Lomen the woman with five children doesn't want to use birth control.
5. Mrs. Bailey denies pain yet she has been crying and is unable to sleep.

---

*See Appendix II for a discussion of correct choices in these exercises.

6. Mr. Jones will be discharged in the morning and his family will be coming for him.
7. There are four steps in the nursing process assessment planning intervention and evaluation.
8. In reviewing the chart the supervisor noticed several errors.
9. Brain stem depression was caused by a tumor.
10. University Hospital offers specialization in Obstetrics, Urology, Neurology, ICU, Pediatrics and Oncology.
11. She was described by the psychologists as an overly protective mother.
12. Well child care can be provided by a family nurse practitioner or a pediatric nurse practitioner.
13. Knowing the prognosis was poor the health care team requested a meeting with the family.
14. Nursing has struggled to attain professional status but is hampered by the entry into practice issue.
15. The health history includes demographic data the past health history the family history a review of systems sociological and psychological data and information concerning the present state of the client.
16. After the medication was given the patients behavior became extremely agitated.
17. Nursing like any other profession requires dedication and commitment.
18. The World Health Organization defines health as a state of complete physical mental and social well being not merely the absence of disease.
19. The Primary Care Clinic which is run by nurses is located on East Main.
20. In my opinion nurses who work in primary care settings need physical assessment skills.
21. The following areas will be covered in this course interviewing skills data collection techniques used in physical assessment and proper documentation of findings.
22. An adequate diet includes the proper balance of

carbohydrates protein and fat.

23. Because it was the students first day on the unit the instructor remained close at hand.

24. Mr. Morrison who was admitted for gall bladder surgery has developed chest pain.

25. The students have performed the tasks in the skills lab but they still require supervision on the nursing unit.

26. Procedures which require invasive techniques are harder to perform.

27. Sensing the tension in the staff the head nurse called a meeting.

28. A thorough assessment includes the physical psychological and psychosocial aspects of the client.

29. After assessing the clients health status the nurse documented her findings.

30. Language poverty and cultural beliefs can be barriers to health care delivery for ethnic people.

CHAPTER 3

Planning: The Heart of the Writing Process

WHY PLANNING?

Many people associate competence in writing with the skills reviewed in Chapter 2. But such skills are equivalent to the techniques of nursing care. Proficiency in bedmaking or giving injections would not in itself signify a competent nurse. Nursing requires an understanding of the process of health care delivery and an ability to implement that process effectively in specific care-giving situations. There is an analogy in written communication. Nurses who can write *correctly* have achieved useful skills, but they must also learn how to plan a writing task and implement that plan effectively if they are to be truly competent writers. Chapters 3 and 4 delineate these facets of the writing process.

Planning is a key phase in both the nursing process and the writing process, but there are many important differences between planning for nursing intervention and planning a writing project. The Nursing Care Plan is the form of planning basic to the nursing process. It is a formalized, systematic approach to care which is developed as the result of an initial assessment. The care plan of the nurse in the clinical setting is more concise than the educational care plan of the student nurse, but both are designed to be read by other health-care professionals. The plan in nursing care is intended as a document that makes visible the enactment of the nursing process. It is viewed by regulatory agencies as an indicator of the type and quality of care given and is an important record in the clinical setting.

As in the nursing process, planning is integral to the writing process, but it is in practice most often less systematic and more individualized. One major difference is that the writing plan is not intended to be a separate and finished "product" like the Nursing Care Plan. In writing, the plan is the blueprint or design which is only a *tool* for development of the letter, report, or article. In school you are often asked to write and "hand in" a formal outline or plan, but that is part of the educational process rather than the writing process. The instructor wants to examine the writer's ability to plan since many problems in written communication are the result of faulty planning. In professional writing, the writer's plan is not a finished product in itself; it is a personal guide for the writer. The plan's form, then, will most often depend on the type and length of the writing task and the experience of the writer.

Planning focuses on actions to be initiated, and not all planning involves a written record. Most nurse-to-nurse oral communication involves informal plans for health care delivery.

- "Can you help me turn Mr. Sayres at 11 AM?"
- "Will you take Mr. Lowery's history before you pass meds, or do you want me to do it?"
- "What time is Mrs. Weiss supposed to be ambulated?"

In the clinical care setting, a team leader's routine will include attention to formal nursing care plans but may also involve "mental plans" for how to:

- Try to get the vital signs finished by 4 PM to have time to spend answering Mr. Palermo's questions about his colostomy.
- Complete the assessment on the new admission in 542 by 7 PM.
- Find time to show Steve how to irrigate Miss Schmidt's feeding tube.

The actual interventions may be part of the formal care plan, but the implementation of that plan requires further informal and flexible planning.

The same is true of writing. All writing is planned, but very often that plan is part of a mental process or a very informal series of notes decipherable only by the writer. Figure 3-1 illustrates the "planning" for the first two pages of this chapter. Do not try to explain all the items in terms of the finished pages you are reading; some ideas were abandoned in the planning stage, many in subsequent revisions.

While planning **techniques** in writing can consist of several elements (some careful thinking, a few brief notes, a rough diagram of interrelated ideas, or a carefully worded series of statements— depending on the scope of the writing project and the temperament work habits, and experience of the writer), **the process of planning,** like the writing process itself, consists of several important phases with which every writer should be familiar.

Before discussing planning in detail, it is important to note that, frequently, nursing students have a minimal need to plan their writing. Because nursing education emphasizes preparation in methodology, writing assignments tend to be extremely prescriptive, thereby limiting the writer's options. For example, with an assignment to "write a paper exploring an issue in current nursing practice," it is not uncommon to receive instructions to:

1. Identify and describe the issue.
2. Present the historical development of the issue.
3. Identify and analyze the major factors involved.
4. Take a stand on the issue and defend the position.

Clearly, much of the planning has already been included in this assignment. However, you will not always be writing in response to such specific directions. As a professional nurse you will have many writing projects that require you to implement the entire planning process. Some aspects of this process will be valuable for you in making even very prescriptive assignments better papers; the entire process is important to be able to write with skill and ease in any setting.

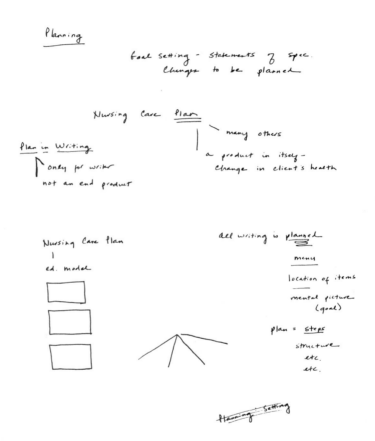

Figure 3-1. Planning in action!

THE PLANNING PROCESS

As in the nursing process, planning in writing is dependent on the initial assessment. That is, all writers must refer to their basic rhetorical position, the "writer's triangle" (see Fig. 1-1) to assess the nature of their subject and the relation to their audience—what is being written and to whom. Here the nursing student and the graduate nurse both have an advantage. Their subject and audience are usually clearly defined, whether the writing project is a class paper, a letter of application, or an article for a journal. It is from this awareness of the nature of the writer's relationship to both subject and audience that the process of planning is initiated.

In the nursing process, two of the central activities of planning are goal setting and the subsequent statement of activities. There is a close parallel in the planning of writing.

Goal Setting

All writing tasks should be initially summarized in one clear statement of purpose. It is simply stating the basic rhetorical position (the "writer's triangle") in *specific terms*.

Examples:

1. I am writing a report for the County Health Department to summarize and evaluate the services provided by Blue Mountain Mental Health Agency.
2. I am writing a paper for my Nursing 192 class exploring the Entry Into Practice issue in nursing.
3. I am writing about our technique for alleviating the pain of sprains in the ED at Mercy Hospital for the "Clinical Highlights" section of *RN* magazine.
4. I am writing a letter of application for an advertised position as an RN with extensive ICU-CCU experience.

Just as in the nursing process all nursing actions develop from the specific goals, all planning in writing should be generated from the specific statement of the goal. The goal is not quite the same thing as the controlling idea or thesis, but the two are closely related.

Examples:

Goal	Controlling Idea
I am writing an extended definition of "health" for my Fundamentals of Nursing class.	One really never comes to an acceptable and complete definition of health.
I am writing to apply for the position of supervisor of the pediatric and adolescent care unit at Memorial Hospital.	I am highly qualified; I have had 16 years' experience in pediatric nursing, including seven years in administration.
I am writing an article for *AJN* about how I think nursing can best serve the handicapped client.	Handicapped individuals should not have their disability unduly emphasized when being treated for an unrelated condition in a nonspecialized health care facility.

All writers should be aware of their goal and the controlling idea which informs their presentation. For the inexperienced writer this means writing both items down so that they can be examined for accuracy, relevance, and clarity. Many pages of unsuccessful writing are often the result of failure to begin with these preliminary but essential steps. Most often the goal is apparent before the controlling idea (though not always), and sometimes there can be a lot of analysis before the controlling idea is established. This is a phase known as *prewriting* because although it may, in fact, involve quite a lot of writing—or none at all—it is a preliminary and preparatory step, a part of developing the plan, and not part of the actual article, essay, or letter which will be the final result of the writing process.

Prewriting
Sometimes called brainstorming, sometimes known as free-writing, prewriting is a process of freely associating facts, opinions, and ideas relative to your overall goal in an attempt to arrive at a

controlling idea, the single concept you want to present in your writing. If the writing project involves research, the research has usually been completed by this stage of planning. Prewriting is a process of synthesizing the writer's knowledge and experience into an informed position. Some writers make lists, others simply generate information in random phrases and sentences. Whatever the technique used, the purpose of prewriting is to arrive at the **controlling idea** or **thesis.** This is the most important single part of your writing project. From this statement all supporting information should be generated. We might diagram the process as in Figure 3-2.

Controlling Idea

The controlling idea in writing is analogous to the goal in the Nursing Care Plan. From that goal, the nurse plans actions to effect the desired change. So, for example, the goal:

Increase length of intervals of sleep at night

might result in the following nursing orders:

1. Provide warm, sedative bath at 9:30 PM and follow c̄ warm milk.
2. Assist to bed and give sedative backrub.

In like manner, the supporting details in your writing must develop in response to your controlling idea (as shown in Fig. 3-2).

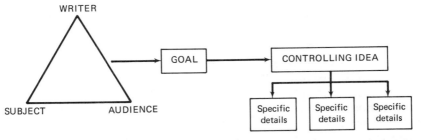

Figure 3-2. The controlling idea in writing. From this statement all supporting information should be generated.

Let's illustrate this process with a specific example. We have been asked to write a brief and informal essay for a patient education pamphlet on juvenile diabetic care and have been assigned the subject of adolescent diabetics. We understand that our audience will not be health care professionals but clients, probably parents of diabetic children. From our professional knowledge and experience, we develop a controlling idea that we think will be informative and valuable for that audience.

Controlling idea   Adolescent diabetics should be taught to assume total responsibility for their care.

As we ask ourselves *why* we think this, we generate the following support sentences in response to that controlling idea:

1. The disease must not become a part of the possible "adolescent rebellion" of this age group.
2. Adolescents are self-sufficient enough to handle the physical care necessary for their condition.
3. Adolescence is a natural stage of separation and self-awareness.
4. Adolescents are developing autonomy in life style.

(Note that each statement is written as *a complete sentence.* Ignore the impulse to write just words or phrases at this stage of the process. Forcing yourself to write complete sentences will help clarify your thinking and save you extra work later on in the process.)

After we've written these statements, we check them to see if they are indeed specifically related to the controlling idea. Just as you would not write a nursing order unrelated to the patient's actual or possible problems, you don't write any ideas on the subject that are unrelated to the controlling idea.

Next, we examine each of these statements as possible **topic sentences,** that is, sentences from which we can develop an entire paragraph. Is each of our supporting statements broad enough to allow for development and is each a distinctly different topic? As we look at the statements, 3 and 4 seem to be so closely related that they would become part of one paragraph, so we combine them as:

3. Adolescence is a natural stage of developing autonomy.

The writer should then ask:

"Does everything I will say fit under one of these sentences, or will I need to generate more topic sentences to cover additional ideas?"

Remember, more can be added later. A plan is not a permanent commitment, but it is easier to work with your ideas when there are four sentences written than when there are four pages—or 40. If the writer is satisfied that the complete development of each of the topic sentences will adequately present the controlling idea, the next question is the order of the paragraphs.

Logical Order

As we look at the sentences we've generated, we try to determine if there seems to be any clear order dictated by the material, ie., what should come first, second, etc. Unless dictated as part of a writing assignment, this sequence is the writer's option and is very much an aspect of the "creativity" that instructors try to call forth from students. Since all the information is related to the controlling idea, there are no rules to follow in organizing effectively. Some topics seem to naturally fall into a chronological pattern, others into a spatial format. The order chosen should enhance the writer's purpose as much as possible. If you are undecided about the arrangement of your information, a good procedure is to write your topic sentences in different sequences to try to see which order seems to present a natural evolution of your subject as you would like to present it to your audience. In this case, we decide to present our ideas in this way:

Controlling idea	Adolescent diabetics should be taught to assume total responsibility for their care.
Topic sentence #1	Adolescents are self-sufficient enough to handle the physical care necessary for their condition.

Topic sentence #2   Adolescence is a natural stage of developing autonomy.

Topic sentence #3   The disease must not become a part of the possible "adolescent rebellion" of this age group.

Our essay is now at the stage illustrated by the diagram in Figure 3-3, the basic pattern of all discourse. Remember that *all choices are tentative*; at the planning stage we are always writing and rescanning with intervention in mind. The basic structure of our essay is now completed, but we have only four sentences! The next action is to develop each paragraph, keeping in mind that the topic sentence may always be altered or changed if necessary.

Paragraph Development

The most important concept to keep in mind in relation to writing paragraphs is *unity*—a paragraph presents *one* idea. All sentences in the paragraph are intended to support, develop, explain, or illustrate the one idea that the writer intends to convey . . . the idea expressed in the topic sentence. As topic sentences are developed, they are modified, sometimes changed completely, as the writer's thoughts develop and are articulated. Development of the individual paragraphs and putting them together as a coherent whole in support of the controlling idea involves much intervention and rewriting as the writer attempts to give specific voice to the plan. Let's look at our completed essay (the topic sentences are italicized) and discuss some of the processes that bring us to this point.

Independence for the Adolescent Diabetic

Juvenile diabetes is a family disease. The patient is never the only client. Most children who are diagnosed as diabetics are hospitalized for control of the disease and education. But equally important is the care and education of parents who may suffer guilt, anxiety, and fear, and who may have to assume much, if not all, responsibility for the child's daily care. However, such health care should complement the child's natural

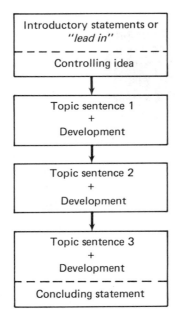

Figure 3-3. The basic pattern of expository discourse. The chain of paragraphs is either shortened or lengthened depending on the scope of the thesis, but the essential structure remains unchanged.

physical and psychological development, so it is important to understand why *adolescent diabetics should be taught to assume total responsibility for their own health care.*

The personal care demanded by diabetes is crucial and exacting, and this care can often be a burden to parents of juvenile diabetics. Depending on the child's age, the parents' responsibilities may include either doing or supervising regular urine testing, providing the proper diet, and administering the medication as ordered. Few children of elementary school age, for example, are able to understand the complexity of the care or manage the injections easily. *Adolescent diabetics, however, are old enough to manage all the physical care needed for their condition.* They not only are able to understand the physiology of the disease, but are physically able to administer their own medication, plan and follow the proper diet, and respond to the warning signs and symptoms of the disease.

Allowing adolescents to assume responsibility for their

own care is not advocated simply for the relief of parents but for the welfare of the young person. *Adolescence is a stage of naturally developing autonomy.* Young people are searching for their own identity as men and women in society. It is a time when there is a closer association with peers and peer values than with family, a time of burgeoning self-awareness, and a time of forging new life styles.

Unfortunately, the impulse toward separation from parents can cause a conflict with personal care. The adolescent's movement toward autonomy and role experimentation sometimes precludes the regularity of life style important to diabetic care. In addition, the peer involvement common to this age group precludes "being different" in any way. The strong pressure to conform can be a problem for the diabetic in social situations. Above all, if the care is seen as a parental priority, it may be rejected simply as part of the separation process. *It is important to separate the diabetes from other parental pressures lest the young person neglect care as a form of self-assertion.* The adolescent who feels psychologically independent should not be made to feel unnecessarily physically dependent by parental overprotection in the area of health. If the parents are able to transfer both management and concern for the disease to the young person while remaining supportive and living, the diabetic will be enabled to incorporate the disease into his or her own identity and life style.

You will note that the topic sentence is not always the first sentence in the paragraph, though the topic sentence comes first in the writing process. During the development of the individual ideas, considerations of style and coherence often alter the order of presentation among the sentences and dictate the placement of the topic sentence. Note, too, that the *usual* position of the controlling idea is near the end of the first paragraph. This insures that the writer provides the reader with some type of introduction or "lead-in" to the central idea. Often this first paragraph is the *last* thing written.

Coherence

Coherence in writing is the partner of unity. A paragraph is *unified* when all of its sentences point in the same direction, follow the same line of thought; a paragraph is *coherent* when that unity seems smooth and natural. Coherence is the mechanical way in which sentences are intertwined to "flow" one into the other. If you have ever seen the children's game "Barrel of Monkeys" it perfectly illustrates coherence. The monkeys are linked together by their arms to form a string, like links on a chain. You provide coherence in your essay when you find means for sentences to lead one into the other.

The fact that the paragraph or essay or letter is all about one thing (the controlling idea) provides a certain amount of internal coherence, but often it is necessary to reinforce that unity. When you read your prose and it sounds "choppy," that's a sign that you need to attend to coherence. There are three practical ways of adding coherence to your writing:

1. Repetition of key words or concepts.
2. Pronoun reference.
3. Transitional words.

Each of these techniques provides a pointer between what's to follow and what has come before. We've marked in boldface the use of techniques to provide coherence in our essay on adolescent diabetics and indicated with numbers the type of emphasis used (as listed above).

Independence for the Adolescent Diabetic

Juvenile diabetes is a family disease. The patient is never the only client. Most children who are diagnosed as diabetics are hospitalized for control of the disease and education. **But** equally important is the care and education of parents who may suffer guilt, anxiety, and fear, and who may have to assume much, if not all, responsibility for the child's daily care.

^{3}
However, such health care should complement the child's

natural physical and psychological development, so it is

important to understand why adolescent diabetics should be

taught to assume total responsibility for their own health care.

The personal care demanded by diabetes is crucial
^{1}
and exacting, and **this care** can often be a burden to

parents of juvenile diabetics. Depending on the child's age,

the parents' responsibilities may include either doing or super-

vising regular urine testing, providing the proper diet, and

administering the medication as ordered. Few children of ele-
^{3}
mentary school age, **for example**, are able to understand the

complexity of the care or manage the injections easily. Adoles-
^{3}
cent diabetics, **however**, are old enough to manage all the
^{2}
physical care needed for their condition. **They** not only are able

to understand the physiology of the disease, but are physically

able to administer their own medication, plan and follow the

proper diet, and respond to the warning signs and symptoms of

the disease.
^{1}
Allowing adolescents to assume responsibility for

their own care is not advocated simply for the relief of parents but for the welfare of the young person. Adolescence is a stage of naturally developing autonomy. Young people are searching for their own identity as men and women in society.

2

It is a time when there is a closer association with peers and peer values than with family, a time of burgeoning self aware- ness, and a time of forging new life styles.

3   1

Unfortunately, the impulse toward separation from parents can cause a conflict with personal care. The adoles- cent's movement toward autonomy and role experimentation sometimes precludes the regularity of life style important to

3

diabetic care. **In addition**, the peer involvement common to this age group precludes "being different" in any way. The strong pressure to conform can be a problem for the dia-

3

betic in social situations. **Above all**, if the care is seen as a parental priority, it may be rejected simply as part of the sepa- ration process. It is important to separate the diabetes from other parental pressures lest the young person neglect care as a form of self-assertion. The adolescent who feels psychologi- cally independent should not be made to feel unnecessarily physically dependent by parental overprotection in the area of health. If the parents are able to transfer both management

and concern for the disease to the young person while remain-

ing supportive and loving, the diabetic will be enabled to incor-

porate the disease into his or her own identity and life style.

This explanation of planning may not change your own composing habits—nor is it intended to, unless you find your own habits
inadequate. Knowing how planning functions as part of the writing
process does not mean that you must follow this model step by step
in everything you write. It means that there is a process basic to
writing which you can depend on to facilitate or improve your own
writing. Many people write clearly and fluently seemingly "automatically," without any formal planning. This only means that
they have internalized the process and are applying it intuitively.

For example, here is an actual letter written by a staff nurse on
her own inititive without reference to any formal method of planning. The writer planned mentally and revised as needed until the
letter sounded like what she wanted to say.

Dear Ms. McCaffery:

I read your article on pain control in the October issue of
Nursing 80 and found it very informative. You dealt **however,**
only with patients in acute post-surgical or post-traumatic
pain. As nurses on a 75-bed orthopedic unit, my coworkers and
I often have to deal with patients in chronic pain, and **we**
frequently discuss our feelings about the use of narcotics for
these patients. *Most often I find nurses questioning narcotic
orders, as you describe in your article, but it is on orders for
patients with chronic rather than acute pain.*

*Our team conferences on pain control often revolve around
two types of chronic patient we see most often.* **The first** is the
patient who appears in acute pain, who takes narcotics as often
as ordered for a month or more, and who is discharged without
any appreciable change in condition. Diagnostic studies show
no abnormality. **The second type** of patient takes his medica-

tions as often as possible but does not appear uncomfortable. This patient ambulates in the hallways, laughs and jokes with the staff, etc.

We have discussed **your article** in team conferences and, as a result, I think we all feel more comfortable about medication for post-op patients. **However,** *we still cannot resolve our questions about the chronic pain patients.* How do you determine whether the symptoms are physiological or whether they are a means for the patient to receive drugs in a legitimate fashion? I am not suggesting that the patients are consciously faking, but isn't it possible that there is a point when the body feels pain as a means to an end—that is, narcotic medication?

It would be very helpful to our team, and I'm sure to other nurses as well, if you could address this issue of chronic pain.

Sincerely,

Vicki W. Conner, R.N.

You may write many of your own letters and brief reports with the same informal planning Mrs. Conner employed. But as we check this letter against the general pattern for all writing (Fig. 3-3), we can identify the essential elements—controlling idea, topic sentences (italics), unified paragraphs, logical order, coherence (boldface). Planning is not only to help you organize your thoughts and ideas, it can also be used to check what you have said to be sure you've been clear and logical. If you understand the components of planning, when your writing doesn't "sound right" to you, you know the elements to check for to see where you've gone awry. To understand the process is to enable you to write with skill and care in a variety of situations.

More Formal Planning

The procedure we've presented for generating ideas and topics from a controlling idea is basic to planning all writing. However, sometimes a more formal plan is needed. This is especially true when:

1. The paper or project will be very long and detailed;
2. The subject is extremely complex and/or abstract;
3. The paper or project is part of the educational process; that is, much of the learning is in the plan developed by the student.

This more formal plan is usually presented as a **topic outline**. (The more informal model we used for the essay on adolescent diabetics is known as a sentence outline.)

For example, in one philosophy of nursing seminar, students received instructions for the term project as follows:

"Develop a theoretical framework for your nursing practice from the concepts discussed in this course."

Two students wrote their outlines as follows:

Student A	Student B
I. Presentation of nursing practice	I. Philosophy of nursing practice
II. Presentation of relevant professional concepts	II. Relationship of philosophy to practice
III. Development of philosophy of nursing	III. Integration of philosophy with practice
IV. Effect of philosophy on clinical practice	IV. Effect of philosophy on practice

Each student developed a different approach to the assignment, but in each case the plan is logical and thorough. There is no one correct way to present information. The principal criterion in evaluating a formal plan such as this is "Does the plan present the subject in a logical and coherent sequence?"

The closest analogy to this type of topic planning can be observed in the Table of Contents of a book. The Table of Contents reflects the careful planning the author has done to insure that the information will be coherently presented and logically developed. Figure 3-4 illustrates the segment of a book's Table of Contents for a unit on the nursing process. Note how the entire unit is divided into

UNIT II	
THE NURSING PROCESS	
Chapter 6	
Introduction to the Nursing Process	107
Problem Solving	107
Critical Thinking	108
Creativity	108
Their Role Together	108
Nursing Process	108
Phases of the Process	108
Assessment	108
Planning	109
Intervention	109
Evaluation	109
Interrelationship of Phases	109
Versatility of the Nursing Process	110
Recording and the Nursing Process	110
The Chart	111
Approaches to Recording	112
The Traditional Approach	112
The Problem-Oriented Record	113
SOAPIE	114
General Guidelines for Effective Recording	115
Notes	119
Selected References	119
Chapter 7	
Assessment	121
Process of Assessment	121
Subjective and Objective Data	121
Organization and Analysis of Data	122
Assessment Factors	122
Assessment Tools	123
Observation	124
Observation, a Conscious, Purposeful Process	124
Interviewing	125
The Directive Approach	125
The Nondirective Approach	125
A "Combined" Technique	126
Interview Conditions	126
Feeling at Ease	126
Process Recording	127
Achieving Effectiveness	127
The Nursing History	127
Psychosocial Assessment	127
Psychomotor Skills	140
Physical Assessment	140
Inspection	140
Palpation	140
Percussion	141
Auscultation	142
Diagnostic Tests	142
Medical Diagnosis and Physician's Orders	144
Assessment—An Ongoing Process	145
Selected References	145
Chapter 8	
Nursing Diagnosis	153
Identifying Elements of the Nursing Diagnosis	153
Nursing Diagnosis Defined	154
Types of Nursing Diagnoses	154
Purposes of Nursing Diagnoses	154
Differentiation Between Nursing	

Figure 3-4. A segment of a book's Table of Contents for a unit on the nursing process. (From Brill, EL Kilts, DF: *Foundations for Nursing.* New York, Appleton-Century-Crofts, 1980, pp xiii-siv. Reprinted with permission.)

Figure 3-4. (Continued)

chapters dealing with phases of the process and then further subdivided into aspects of those phases. In a like manner, most longer pieces of writing (beyond 1000 words or four typewritten pages) usually need a formal plan that will enable the writer to present the material in a logical and coherent sequence. The nurse's research report, for example, is usually presented in an eight-stage format described in Chapter 6. This is the acceptable professional method for reporting research data. However, in other types of projects, journal articles, or books the plan is more flexible and is the responsibility of the writer.

Example:

Topic: Modern Nursing Practice: New Roles for Nurses

I. Causes
A. Advances in technology

      B. Redefinition of nursing as a profession
      C. Needs of clients
  II. Models
      A. Primary care nurse
      B. Independent practitioner
      C. Clinical specialist
  III. Consequences
      A. Legal changes
      B. Education developments
      C. Self-evaluation

This is a standard topic outline. It provides the writer with a clear structure and guidance, assuring that he or she does not get "lost"— as, for example, in writing about primary care nursing and forgetting that the overall topic includes *three* new roles for nurses. The outline is designed to provide guidance and direction without being restrictive. The outline may be expanded depending upon the writer's need for specificity. For example, note how "Section III. B. Education developments" may be expanded with more specific details:

  III. Consequences
      B. Education developments
         1. Certification programs
            a. Midwifery
            b. Gerontologic nursing
            c. School nursing
         2. Master's degree programs
            a. Nursing practice
            b. Nursing education
            c. Nursing administration
         3. Doctoral programs
            a. Nursing research
            b. Nursing education
            c. Nursing administration

The idea is not to make a "perfect" outline, but to provide yourself with the amount of structure you need to direct your writing. Only you know exactly how much outlining you require for any given topic. Figure 3-5 illustrates the standard formal outline. Where your knowledge is thorough, you may need only the briefest topic headings for guidance (Roman numbers only, perhaps); in some areas you may need a more exhaustive listing. The writer's needs determine the length of the outline. The outline must not restrict or overwhelm the actual writing, and only the writer can provide the proper balance. Outline as much as you need to for guidance and direction but do not feel obligated to outline beyond that point.

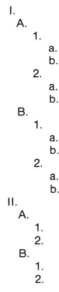

Figure 3-5. The formal outline form. Note that the principle is that wherever there's a 1 or I, there must be a 2 or II. Wherever there's an A or a, there must be a B or b. However, this basic plan could be extended to any length the topic requires—all the way to Z and indefinitely numerically!

EXERCISES

I.   For each **goal,** develop a **controlling idea or thesis:**

A.   I am designing a program for my Nursing 292 class to change health behavior.

      B. I am writing an essay for *RN* magazine on the importance of the Nursing Care Plan.

      C. I am applying for a grant to establish a geriatric outpatient clinic in our hospital.

      D. I am writing a letter to the editor of *The New York Times* about the need for the public to be more aware of nursing as a *profession.*.

II. For any *one* of the controlling ideas you developed in Exercise I, write *three* topic sentences.

III. Develop any *one* of the three sentences you generated in Exercise II. Evaluate your paragraph for unity.

IV. Evaluate each of the following paragrahs for unity. Correct as needed:

      A. Statistics show that suicide in young children is on the rise. In 1955, there were 0.4/100,000 deaths in children 10–14 years old. In 1975, the number had risen to 1.2/100,000 deaths in the same age group. Something must be done about this, and it is primarily a parental responsibility. In the late 1960s, it was estimated that 7–10 percent of children seen in psychiatric clinics had suicidal symptoms, whereas in 1980, one New York clinic reported that of 39 children randomly chosen, 33 percent had contemplated, threatened, or tried suicide.

      B. Patient education is an important aspect of holistic health care, but unfortunately many hospitals do not provide specialized nurses for this service. Each staff nurse is expected to provide thorough patient education as part of his or her routine duty. It is vital that the administration provide in-service training and team conferences to support nurses in this area, so that patient education will not be neglected in favor of more pressing responsibilities.

      C. Epilepsy is a chronic neurologic disorder which, in most cases, requires continuous anticonvulsant therapy. Because the disease is essentially incurable, the client must be adequately educated for lifetime selfcare. The nurse is frequently the the principal educator for the epileptic. Nurses also provide much patient education for maternity clients. There are many misconceptions about epilepsy which the nurse/educator must be sure to correct.

V.   Identify and evaluate the **coherence** in this paragraph written by a sophomore-level student nurse:

Now let us take a look at the 1900s when the social awareness of the problem of the handicapped gained momentum in this country. This awareness resulted in the organization of special conferences on the welfare of the handicapped child and the opening of clinics and centers for their treatment. World Wars I and II saw the accompanying of physical reconditioning of crippled soldiers with the rehabilitation of the handicapped. They were also covered under the same type of medical care which has today developed into physical therapy. Federal legislation had been enacted following World War I to provide certain medical benefits to disabled veterans. The first law providing for assistance to civilians with disabling injuries was passed in 1920. From the 1940s to the present there has been a steady growth of services to the handicapped as the result of private, state, and federal assistance. One main example is the establishment of special hospitals for certain kinds of handicapped individuals.

VI. Write the formal outline *you* need for an essay on one of the following topics:
   A.   Recent Changes in Nursing Practice
   B.   Wellness Promotion
   C.   Communication Skills for Nurses
   D.   The Public Image of the Nurse

CHAPTER 4

Writing Well: Implementing Planning Effectively

Writing Effective Paragraphs

Any written discourse, from a class essay to a grant application, research report, or journal article involves a basic **plan,** as explained in Chapter 3. During the next phase of the writing process, the writer *develops* the plan. Each of the ideas introduced must be defined, illustrated, explained, or otherwise presented more fully. Individual paragraphs are developed from each of the supporting details in the plan. It is important to understand that each paragraph is an individual unit of thought that contributes to the overall essay—a building block of meaning. *All* paragraphs must have **unity** (be about one dominant idea) and **coherence** (individual sentences connect), and one way to insure this is to develop the paragraph with care. Often the topic sentence will dictate a pattern of development, but a useful technique for developing *any* paragraph is to ask questions about the topic sentence.

Who? What? Why? Where?
How? In what way?
What examples from experience?
What examples from reading?

Obviously all the questions will not be applicable to every topic sentence, but note, for example, how a writer can use these questions to develop a topic sentence:

Topic Sentence: Silence can be an effective technique in therapeutic communication.

Who?	Not applicable
What?	Not applicable
How?	Through silence the client is provided with an opportunity to collect and organize his or her thoughts and/or reflect upon what has preceded in the communication.
When?	When appropriate
Why?	Silence adds trust in the helper/client relationship. Through silence the helper establishes that he or she is willing to be with the client and that verbalization is not a requirement for their being together. Silence is an asset to the helper in establishing an atmosphere of trust.
Where?	Not applicable

To this list of basic questions, the writer may add *examples from experience* and/or *examples from reading*. For this topic sentence, the writer wrote an example from his experience as a cardiac care nurse:

In my nursing practice, I frequently have to be supportive of the relatives of patients who are acutely ill and in imminent danger of death. In many cases these relatives want neither information nor advice but are trying to come to terms with the situation. I have found that silence is particularly effective at such times. I try to be with the people concerned without projecting any of my own feelings inappropriately. Not using words is helpful in such situations: often touch or gesture is enough to say, "I care."

The writer's final paragraph reads:

> Used effectively, silence can be helpful in therapeutic communication. With silence the helper can establish a deep level of trust with the client by assuring him or her that verbalization is not a requirement for their being together. The client is provided with an opportunity to collect and organize thoughts and reflect as necessary in the presence of a caring and supportive helper. As a cardiac care nurse who must often care for the concerned relatives of acutely ill patients, I find that sometimes silence is the only way to be present. Often touch or gesture is enough to say "I care."

This entire paragraph is a synthesis of the responses to the basic questions. Compare this paragraph with the following one written on the same topic:

> Silence can be an effective technique in therapeutic communication. The absence of verbalization between nurse and client is often salutary. Silence aids communication in a variety of settings. Every nurse should be aware of the importance of the effective use of silence in communication with clients.

What is the problem with this paragraph? Look at it carefully and you will note that it is developed by *repetition,* a common problem that plagues inexperienced writers. In attempting to provide support for the topic sentence, the writer has only succeeded in repeating that sentence in a variety of different ways. Every paragraph must **develop** the basic idea, so it is vital to avoid stringing together sentences that are merely variations of the topic sentence.

Another problem with paragraph development is illustrated by the following paragraph:

> Silence is an effective technique in therapeutic communication. Clients dislike too much talk; it makes them nervous and uneasy. Many clients who are reluctant to talk about their health problems are put off by the professional's insistent questions or comments. Silence is more important than saying useless words.

In this case, the writer has merely given a series of *unsupported generalizations*. Since the topic sentence is usually a general statement, the task of the remaining sentences is to clarify, explain, define, or otherwise provide the necessary support or explanation for that initial generalization. The writer should not simply multiply general statements. A good rule to remember is that in writing *there is no assertion without evidence*. Do not simply add facts to your topic sentence, *illustrate* it. Each paragraph is responsible for providing the evidence for the claim that paragraph is making. The basic questions to ask of any topic sentence (see p. 75) provide a general guideline for developing paragraphs. Often, however, the topic sentence will indicate a particular pattern of development.

PARAGRAPH PATTERNS

The *pattern* of a paragraph is a distinctive mode of presentation. For example, if you were asked to write a paragraph about how you became interested in nursing, very likely you would write a narrative—i.e., a story. There are many types of paragraph patterns, but the ones that are most directly applicable to nursing education and practice are:

- Generalization with supporting details
- Analysis
- Definition
- Causal analysis
- Process analysis
- Classification

Generalization with Supporting Details

The topic sentence makes some type of claim or assertion, and the balance of the paragraph provides some basis for that claim. The paragraph on silence is an example of this type of paragraph. The following paragraph on documentation is also written according to this most basic pattern:

Documentation is essential to quality health care delivery. Orders transmitted verbally pose too great a risk of error in communication. Written documentation insures a common understanding among all members of the health care team. In addition, proper documentation establishes a record of health care given that can be used evaluatively to determine the quality of the care. Documentation also provides a data base for use in future care giving situations.

Analysis

In analysis the writer focuses on the component parts of the whole as they provide information about the topic under consideration. Nurses should be particularly adept at analysis as it is the process basic to nursing assessment. The following paragraph is an informal analysis:

What are the qualities of an effective nurse? In a survey of various health care professionals, there was common agreement that a nurse must be accepting, supportive, and non-judgmental toward clients. Professional nurses must be able to establish trust with their clients as a basis for the therapeutic relationship. Ideally, the nurse will inspire the client to participate actively in his or her own health care, making the pursuit of optimum wellness a joint endeavor.

Definition

The process of clarifying terms is known as definition. Since nurses so often use specialized vocabulary, it is essential that terms be defined so that there is a common understanding wherever needed. Even terms that might be commonplace at one agency may have a different meaning at another. The following paragraph defines a term as understood in one particular hospital:

At County Hospital we use the term "health care team" to denote a group that consists of 12 to 14 patients, an R.N., an L.P.N., and an aide. The R.N. is always the team leader and is responsible to the resident physician, the attending physician, and the hospital nursing supervisor. However, since the well-being of the patients is the primary goal of the team, there is no status with regard to duties and responsibilities other than

those reserved to the R.N. by law. It is just as common for the
R.N. to give a backrub as an aide.

Causal Analysis

In causal analysis the component parts of a problem or situation
are examined as they point to a current condition as in the following
communication to a psychiatric social worker:

> The client is suffering from an acute depressive reaction
> following the death of her husband three months ago and her
> radical mastectomy two months later. The diagnosis of cancer
> and the subsequent surgery intensified the already established
> depression. The client suffers from insomnia, anorexia, and
> frequent crying spells. Psychiatric intervention is recom-
> mended.

Process Analysis

Process analysis details the steps or stages involved in a process. A
recipe is process analysis in its simplest form, and the following
paragraph explains a more sophisticated process:

> Kübler-Ross has identified five stages in the grief process
> usually associated with death and dying: denial, anger, bar-
> gaining, depression, and acceptance. Denial is the phase when
> the individual rejects the existence of the loss and continues to
> act as if nothing were wrong. Anger occurs with the beginning
> of recognition of the loss. Bargaining is the attempt by the
> individual to make a deal with someone or something to pre-
> vent the loss. Depression occurs when the individual finally
> recognizes the loss, and acceptance occurs when the individual
> recognizes the situation and its implications and begins to
> interact in new ways. These stages are not necessarily sequen-
> tial nor will they all be experienced by everyone. Some individ-
> uals will move to acceptance very rapidly while others will
> never reach it.

Classification

Unlike analysis, to which it is closely related, the paragraph of
classification enumerates the component parts of a system or object

without any specific reference to the whole. Classification usually refers to types or kinds of things, as in the following paragraph about types of surgery:

> There are several types of surgery with which the nurse should be familiar. Emergency surgery is usually performed in life–threatening situations, whereas urgent surgery is usually performed within a day or two after diagnosis. The urgent surgery may also be for a life-threatening situation, but the delay may be to allow the patient's condition to stabilize enough to allow for surgery. There are other required surgeries, but the nature of the condition allows more time—sometimes weeks or months. Elective surgery also needs to be performed, but the condition is such that the surgery may be scheduled at the convenience of the individual and the surgeon.

A word about paragraph patterns—they are not absolutes and rarely does a writer select the pattern before the content. That is, the writer has a subject and purpose first and foremost. In developing that subject, certain patterns of paragraph development may be helpful in conveying the writer's thoughts, and that's why they are chosen. The mature writer should be aware of the major types of paragraph development so that they can be employed when the topic calls for a particular emphasis. Remember, too, that patterns are often varied within individual paragraphs. For example, note the development of the following paragraph:

definition ⟶ ⌈The nursing process is a tool for effecting change in the health status of the client. It is a form of problem solving which has been ⌊adapted to the needs of nursing. The process

classification→ ⌈is composed of a series of phases—assess-⌊ment, planning, intervention, and evalua-

generalization with supporting details ⟶ ⌈tion. These phases are complementary and interdependent. For example, effective planning is dependent on a thorough and accurate assessment. An ineffectively written plan results in inadequate inter-vention. Evaluation will become haphazard

if the individual phases of the process
have been poorly implemented. Effective use
of the process is a dynamic tool for
optimum client care.

While this paragraph might be thought of overall as *descriptive* of the nursing process, there are actually three separate patterns of development employed. Yet the different patterns do not violate the basic nature of the paragraph which, as we described in Chapter 3, requires unity and coherence. The unity in this paragraph is in its description of the nursing process.

In the writing process, implementing the plan effectively means writing individual paragraphs that *support, enhance,* and *illustrate* the ideas presented. Written communication is an instrument to convey thought. Like all instruments, it is only as effective as the skill of the practitioner. There is no magic in putting words on the page that will convey precisely what you want the reader to understand. Like the nursing process, the writing process depends upon the skill with which it is employed, a skill that is the product of both education and experience.

A NOTE ABOUT DRAFTS

Rarely will any written discourse be developed from plan to finished essay in one step. Rescanning and revising—and revising and rescanning, and still more revising—is the usual pattern. Experienced writers are accustomed to the numerous drafts that are required for effective written communication. A business letter may require less revision than a journal article, but every writer must understand that the final phase of the writing process—rereading what one has written and revising as needed—can never be omitted. What makes this phase particularly difficult is that there are no set rules to follow. The writer must simply ask, "Is this what I want to convey?" and, "Is this how I want to convey it?" Any negative response to these questions requires additional revision. In order for writers to develop ability in revising their written discourse, they should become acquainted with the elements of *style.*

Style

WHAT'S STYLE?

We have emphasized writing correctly, planning carefully, and developing the plan. Another element in effective written communication is style. This is a major component in the writing process, but there is often misunderstanding about how it functions. There is a tendency to think of "style" as ornament, something superfluous and essentially frivolous. We commonly use the word *style* in relation to dress or fashion and speak of being "in style," or wearing something "stylish" or in "the latest style." But the *Oxford English Dictionary* reminds us that the word *style* comes from the Latin *stilus,* a pointed instrument for writing, and entered our language as "a way of speaking or writing."

But even as a way of writing, we often think of *style* as something reserved for poets and novelists. After all, professional nurses mainly write straightforward, scientifically based prose—hardly something requiring "style." Yet, just as there is no writing without planning in some form, it is impossible to write without style. For *style* is essentially a matter of the interaction of writers with their audience, as though we concentrated on one leg of that writer's triangle (Fig. 4-1). The question is not whether or not nurses' professional writing will have "style," but whether or not nurses will be in control of their style.

Style begins in the writer's awareness of rhetorical position, the relation to audience and subject—our basic writer's triangle. Style is the enactment of that relationship of writer to audience and subject. Note, for example, this apparently straightforward statement:

Kara Connolly was offered the position of ICU supervisor at County Hospital.

Consider the variations in meaning suggested by several options in word choice. Substitute any of the listed words for the italicized ones and note how the meaning changes.

WRITER

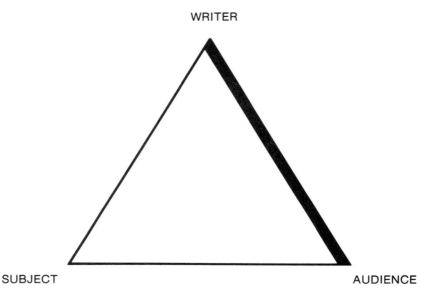

SUBJECT   AUDIENCE

Figure 4-1. Style is concerned with the interaction of writer and audience.

Kara Connolly *was offered* the position of ICU supervisor at County Hospital.

1. promoted to
2. handed
3. assigned

The first substitution suggests merit, the second connotes an unde-served promotion—with a slight suggestion of administrative favoritism, the last implies an obligation rather than a promotion.

Note how Ms. Connolly's response to this promotion is sim-ilarly affected by style when we substitute any of the listed choices for the italicized words.

She said that she *was pleased with* the new position.

1. was overwhelmed by

2. was adjusting to
3. adored

The first choice suggests that Ms. Connolly is very modest—or not too competent, the second conveys the impression that the position requires many changes in Ms. Connolly's professional life, the last gives the impression that she is somewhat immature in her attitude toward her job—or at least in the diction she chooses to express herself.

Diction, the words we choose to convey meaning, is one of the most important ways in which style is established. And, as we have shown, style colors meaning. Since style is such an integral part of the writing process, it is important to be aware of how it functions, for the central question of style is not whether or not it will be used but *how effective* it will be in furthering the writer's purpose. And the effectiveness of the style determines the effectiveness of the writing as a whole.

ASPECTS OF STYLE

Diction or word choice is a basic component of the writer's style. We should choose words appropriate to our subject *and* the audience. For example, this is a letter that student nurse Mary Gale Kovach wrote to her mother concerning her father who is ill with advanced emphysema.

Dear Mom,

Just today I was on the CCU for a while, so I thought I'd write for an update on Dad. Are those episodes of dyspnea still frequent? I hope there's been no sign of peripheral cyanosis, but are you also observing for hypokalemia? You've really got to monitor the action of those diuretics. They reduce the edema, but there are some nontherapeutic residual effects. I'm sure the sodium restriction has effected positive change. Have you been monitoring his fluid intake as well?

I hope you're keeping Dad faithful to his oxygen therapy. It's vital. From what you explained in your last letter, I'd suggest a high semi-Fowler's at night. Keep me posted . . . love to you both,

Mary Gale

Unfortunately, Mary Gale's mother has no background in professional health care, so her concerned daughter's letter is marred by **inappropriate diction.** The choice of words is certainly appropriate to the subject, a patient with emphysema, but this enthusiastic student has used the specialized vocabulary of health care professionals which is inappropriate for this particular audience. (It must be noted here that the patient education movement is very responsive to the needs of patients and their families in assuming ultimate responsibility for their own health and much of the education consists in making the subject—health care—intelligible to the audience—the lay person.)

Another important aspect of style is **level of diction** or **tone.** How do we *sound* to an audience—friendly? angry?—and is that role appropriate to the subject? Both the words we choose and the manner of presentation convey a tonal quality, an implied voice. Listen for the voice in each of the following passages:

1. Congratulations! Now you're a nurse—just out of school and eager to practice your profession. You want to work with other professionals who care about people as you do. You want to continue your professional growth and development. You should come to Harbor Hospital. . . .

2. This is a team, remember? I have three acutely ill patients to care for tonight, and you're asking me about unfilled water pitchers! Do you expect me to do *everything* on this unit myself?

3. Promotion of health practices within the family is a basic goal of family-centered community health nursing. In addition to looking at the overall health and illness patterns of family members, the nurse should also check for the presence or absence of overt health practices.

Now that you are aware of how writing *sounds,* consider the following letter of application. Lawrence Jacobs, an RN whose clinical speciality is psychiatric nursing, has decided to relocate from New York City to Florida, and this is the letter of application he writes:

Phoebe Lewiston, R.N.
Director of Nursing
Sunset Beach Hospital
Clearwater, Florida

Dear Ms. Lewiston,

I'm just the nurse you're looking for! My credentials are superb—BSN and MS in psychology plus five years' clinical experience. I've been supervisor of the psychiatric unit here at Metropolitan Hospital for the past 18 months—pretty much running the entire show here singlehandedly and having a blast. I'm a natural administrator. You'd have trouble finding a better candidate to head your psychiatric unit.

The only reason I'm considering changing positions is to get away from these New York winters. Brrrrr! I could be free to come take a look around there any time you give the word. You'd have a first-class operation with me at the helm.

Best regards,

Larry Jacobs

This is a *correct* letter (i.e., free of errors in punctuation, spelling, or usage) and it's organized, but, of course, it's the wrong **tone** for an applicant-employer communication. Mr. Jacobs writes with the informality Mary Gale should have been using with her mother! The obvious problem with this letter is in the writer-audience relationship, i.e., it's a problem of style. And it's clear from this letter how a problem with style can be devastating, destroying the communication totally.

WHAT STYLE?

Of course, nurses are educated professionals, so such blatant violations of style are relatively rare for them. However, since style is an integral part of the writing process, every nurse should understand how it operates and how it can be controlled for the most effective writing.

The key to style is in the writer-audience relationship, and nurses will most often have one of the following relationships in their professional writing:

- **Professional to other professionals** regarding health care situations and issues (recording, reports, articles for journals, memos, academic theses, books)
- **Personal contact among professionals** (letters of application or recommendation, letters to authors or editors, memos)
- **Professional to laymen and laywomen** (patient education, grant application, articles of general interest, books)

In analyzing **tone,** the basic questions the writer should ask are:

Who am I?   *How should I sound?*

After writing his letter of application, Lawrence Jacobs asked the questions in an effort to find out what was wrong with his letter. He answered, "I am a qualified and competent nurse applying for a position. I want to sound professional and confident (but not boastful or too aggressive) and courteous (but not excessively friendly)." As he rescanned his letter, Mr. Jacobs recognized the wrong tone he had established and rewrote his application as follows:

Phoebe Lewiston, R.N.
Director of Nursing
Sunset Beach Hospital
Clearwater, Florida

Dear Ms. Lewiston:

I am responding to your advertisement in the March issue of the *American Journal of Nursing* for a nurse to head your newly established psychiatric unit. I am currently employed as supervisor of the psychiatric unit at Metropolitan Hospital in New York City, but I plan to relocate to Florida and hope you will consider me for the position available at Sunset Beach Hospital. I have a B.S.N. and an M.S. in psychology. The attached résumé includes other details of my education and professional experience.

My interest in psychiatric nursing developed in nursing school, and during my five years as staff nurse I had broad professional experience. During the past 18 months as head of this unit, I have acquired considerable administrative experience, and I feel qualified to assume the responsibilities you describe in your notice.

My complete dossier is available from the Professional Credentials and Personnel Service of the ANA. Should you desire an interview, I can arrange to be available if given at least five days' notice. I look forward to hearing from you.

Sincerely yours,

Lawrence W. Jacobs

Enc. resume

Obviously, Mr. Jacobs stands a better chance of being granted an interview with his revised letter. We will discuss letters of application in greater detail in Chapter 6, but the point here is that style influences content, and writers must be aware of the effects of style in order to achieve writing proficiency. The way to assess your style is to rescan your writing to *hear* what you sound like. For example, one nurse participated in a project to establish health records for a mental health agency by working with the staff to develop a form to use in conjunction with physician visits. When the proposed form was first submitted to the staff, the nurse reported the results in this paragraph:

There was still something missing on the form. A consent statement from the client was needed that would include consent to release information for the mental health service and a request to obtain information from the physician. With this, the form was complete. The second draft was prepared and presented to the staff. The staff was quite pleased and at that time adopted the form as the means of obtaining health record information for their agency's files.

This is correctly written in terms of the basic mechanics of writing—spelling, punctuation, usage—and the paragraph is unified, but does this discourse *sound* like a professional in a responsible position? The nurse was dissatisfied but was unable to revise effectively. In rescanning, it becomes apparent that the major problem here is an excessive number of words. **Wordiness** is a problem of style which often plagues professionals who are trained to be thorough and clear.

In recording information (charting), nurses are taught to be concise, but often when reporting on a project that involves a process they are so intent on recording each step precisely that they write with an excessive number of words. This makes the discourse seem simplistic. Instead of the two sentences which begin the paragraph, the meaning could be conveyed in one more concisely written statement.

From: There was still something missing on the form. A consent statement from the client was needed that would include consent to release information for the mental health service and a request to obtain information from the physician.

To: The form still needed a consent statement that would include the client's consent to release information for the mental health service and a request to obtain information from the physician.

Seven words were eliminated with the combined sentences, but more important than economy of language is the syntactic sophistication we've achieved. The statement *sounds* more like the writing of an educated professional. Now note how we've combined the final three sentences of the paragraph:

From: With this, the form was complete. The second draft
was prepared and presented to the staff. The staff
was quite pleased and at that time adopted the form
as the means of obtaining health record information
for their agency's files.

To: With the addition of the consent statement, the
staff enthusiastically adopted the form as the means
of obtaining health record information for their
agency's files.

This time we've eliminated 15 words, and again the excision of
excess verbiage enhances the discourse. This is now the language of
one professional to another, the style that the writer was trying to
achieve in the report. The nurse was satisfied that the revision
conveyed her exact meaning more effectively.

In addition to the excess number of words, note that the original paragraph had a repetitive pattern which gave a sense of
clumsiness to the prose:

There *was* still something *missing* on the form. A consent
statement from the client *was needed* that would include consent to release information for the mental health service and a
request to obtain information from the physician. With this,
the form *was complete*. The second draft *was prepared* and
presented to the staff. The staff *was* quite *pleased* and at that
time adopted the form as the means of obtaining health record
information for their agency's files.

The repetition of *was missing, was needed, was complete, was
prepared,* and *was pleased* results in a rhythm to the prose that
almost overwhelms the content. Any such "sameness" in diction,
phrasing, or sentence structure detracts from the presentation—
unless of course it is a *deliberate* attempt to create a rhetorical effect,
as in Abraham Lincoln's famous "for the people, by the people, and
of the people." Most nurses write prose that is intended to communicate directly, clearly, and accurately, so there is no need to emphasize the rhetorical structures that add flourishes and dramatic
effects to written communication.

Most writing handbooks advise writers to avoid the **passive voice** like the proverbial plague. Nurses, however, must learn to understand and use the passive voice effectively. The passive voice (or the passive construction of verbs) is formed by the verb *to be* plus a past participle. In the paragraph we considered, the writer used the passive voice several times:

A consent statement from the client *was needed* . . . .
The second draft *was prepared* . . . .
The staff *was* quite *pleased* . . . .

The passive voice emphasizes the action or object of the action rather than the doer. In this case, the writer *chose* the passive construction, since this is a research report designed to emphasize the actions taken and their results and to de-emphasize the agent involved. However, the passive voice generates a sameness of diction, and the style is weakened unless the writer makes an effort to compensate for this. Effective use of the passive voice is important for writing research reports well (see Chapter 6 for a more detailed discussion of writing research reports).

The opposite of the passive voice is the active voice. Since the normal construction of an English sentence is:

Subject   —   *Verb*   —   *Object*

the active voice's emphasis on the subject makes it more "normal" both in grammar and style. The active voice is, therefore, the preferred verb construction except in those rare instances (research reports, for example) when it is important to de-emphasize the doer of the action. Inappropriate use of the passive voice in correspondence, memos, reports, and essays results in awkwardness of expression and poor style, as you can see in the following examples:

Passive: The report was written by Mrs. Elton.

Active: Mrs. Elton wrote the report.

Passive: Mr. Propkiev was visited by the social worker.

Active:	The social worker visited Mr. Propkiev.
Passive:	The surgery was performed by Dr. LoPresti.
Active:	Dr. LoPresti performed the surgery.

When you are dissatisfied with any discourse you've written, be alert to the possibility that you've used the passive voice inappropriately. As you can see from the examples given, changing to the active voice is both easy and effective. Problems of style are usually harder to identify than to correct, but the best method of identification is to acquire a good "ear" for your own prose.

The principles of good recording—correctness, completeness, and conciseness—are also the basic principles of all good writing. Achieving a concise style is known as writing with economy. Wordiness is often a problem within individual sentences, and we write with economy when we learn to simplify, as in the following examples:

Wordy:	It is known that some women experience discomfort several days prior to menstruation.
Simpler:	Some women experience discomfort several days prior to menstruation.
Wordy:	We implemented the patient education program in order that we might promote cost containment.
Simpler:	We implemented the patient education program to promote cost containment.
Wordy:	In spite of the fact that Mrs. Sellico is considered ambulatory, she refuses to leave her bed.
Simpler:	Although Mrs. Sellico is considered ambulatory, she refuses to leave her bed.

An important factor in avoiding wordiness is proper use of the apostrophe:

Wordy:	The comments from the psychiatrist give encouragement that the prognosis will be good.

Simpler: The psychiatrist's comments suggest a favorable prognosis.

Wordy: The students sought the advice of their clinical instructor in preparing the care plan of Mrs. Stevick.

Simpler: The students sought their clinical instructor's advice in preparing Mrs. Stevick's care plan.

Nurses are particularly prone to the defect of style that is the opposite of wordiness—**choppiness.** In writing care plans and charting in the clinical care setting, nurses naturally develop a writing style that is brief, precise, and correct. However, when those same nurses undertake a writing task that calls for detail and development of ideas, the writing style appropriate to the clinical sett_ng becomes a handicap. The clinical style uses brief, simple sentences or sentence fragments (see Chapter 5, Writing in the Clinical Care Setting), but that style is often "choppy" when used for an article, a thesis, or a grant application. The writer may be able to *develop* his or her thought adequately, but the *sound* may be too clipped or "choppy" for fluency. Note, for example, the sound of this paragraph for a teaching plan:

The newly admitted patient will be visited by a member of the patient education team. The team member will evaluate the acute nature of the patient. The back pain program will be explained. The patient will be invited to participate. The patient's physician will be notified of his or her decision.

In rescanning, the writer noticed the "choppiness," but since this is a professional nurse's communication, he wanted to retain the clear, direct style while also eliminating the choppiness. Observe the revision:

The newly admitted patient will be visited by a member of the patient education team who will evaluate the acute nature of the patient. The back pain program will be explained and the patient invited to participate. The patient's physician will be notified of his or her decision.

By combining sentences, the writer added variety, eliminating the choppiness without sacrificing clarity. Basic to effective sentence combining is an understanding of coordination and subordination.

Coordination is the linking of sentence parts of equal rank or importance. It is best employed when closely related ideas of equal significance are to be expressed. Words, parts of sentences, or whole sentences may be coordinated. The words that customarily coordinate are: *and, but, or, nor, for, yet, so.* Coordination was one of the techniques used by the writer to revise the paragraph above:

Original: The back pain program will be explained. The patient will be invited to participate.

Coordinated: The back pain program will be explained *and* the patient invited to participate.

Examples:

Wordy: The social worker visited Mr. Hickle. She suggested several altenratives for long-term care.

Coordinated: The social worker visited Mr. Hickle. She suggested several alternatives for long-term care.

Wordy: The chest pain may be due to pneumonia. The chest pain may indicate a pulmonary embolism.

Coordinated: The chest pain may be due to pneumonia *or* a pulmonary embolism.

Wordy: Many student nurses need financial aid. The nursing school has inaugurated a system of low-interest loans for qualified students.

Coordinated: Many student nurses need financial aid, *so* the nursing schools has inaugurated a system of low-interest loans for qualified student.

Note that sometimes coordination significantly shortens the sentence groups, but sometimes the number of words remains the same. However, in all cases coordination improves the "flow" of thought and helps overcome the "choppiness."

Subordination is the linking together of "unequal" ideas. In any written discourse all comments are not of equal value. There will be asides and explanations for the reader that add to or comment on the main ideas being expressed. The writer correctly *subordinates* such details. Notice how subordination not only helped the writer overcome "choppiness" in his paragraph, but actually expressed his meaning more accurately:

> *Original:*   The newly admitted patient will be visited by a member of the patient education team. The team member will evaluate the acute nature of the patient.
>
> *Subordinated:*   The newly admitted patient will be visited by a member of the patient education team who will evaluate the acute nature of the patient.

Since the important point is the visit of the team member and that visit is directly related to patient evaluation, the writer's intent is reflected more accurately with subordination than with two separate sentences. Revision for style should not sacrifice meaning; done properly it will enhance and clarify meaning. The words that usually subordinate are: *as, before, because, although, until, that, if, unless, since, when, who, which, while.*

Observe how both fluency and accuracy are developed through subordination in the following examples:

> *Wordy:*   I am the mother of small children, I prefer to work the 3-11 shift.
>
> *Subordinated:*   *Because* I am the mother of small children, I prefer to work the 3-11 shift.
>
> *Wordy:*   Superficial vasoconstriction can be assessed by touch. The skin usually feels cool to the touch.

Subordinated: *With* superficial vasoconstriction, the skin usually feels cool to the touch.

Wordy: Soaks are often applied to a body area where there is an open wound. Sterile technique is maintained and sterile supplies are used.

Subordinated: *When* soaks are applied to a body area where there is an open wound, sterile technique is maintained and sterile supplies are used.

HOW IS EFFECTIVE STYLE ACHIEVED?

As you examine your own writing, it may appear to you that it needs more fluency, needs to "sound" better, but you are not quite sure how to achieve that style which the writers of the texts and journal articles you read seem to have mastered. Take heart. Style is achieved partially through experience but mainly through vigilance. Just as you learn to assess a client, state the health problems, and write appropriate nursing orders, you must learn to assess your written communication, identify the writing problems, and intervene appropriately. Too often inexperienced writers are overwhelmed by the polished prose of some published writer and feel they cannot possibly measure up. But good writing is not any more automatic than good nursing. It is a product of a *learned*, problem-solving process. Just as evaluation is an important stage in the nursing process, revision is a vital part of the writing process.

It is important to know the elements of the writing process to be able to diagnose the problems and intervene accordingly. Just as every pain in the lower right quadrant is not necessarily appendicitis, not every problem in writing is one of style. Problems in style can usually be identified by the fact that the writer is satisfied with the content and organization but knows that it just doesn't "sound right." Figure 4-2 illustrates the basic questions about style that writers should ask about their writing. Use this as a resource for evaluating your style.

In a consideration of style, a word must be said about the

A. **TONE** (How does the writer sound?)
    1. Is the tone appropriate to the audience?
    2. Is the tone appropriate to the subject?
    3. Is the tone the same throughout the writing?

B. **DICTION**
    1. Is the word choice appropriate to the audience and subject?
    2. Is the level of diction consistent?
    3. Is the level of diction appropriate (i.e., neither too formal nor informal)

C. **SYNTAX**
    1. Is there too much wordiness?
       a. Should some sentences be combined?
       b. Should some individual sentences be shortened with the elimination of excess words?
    2. Are there repetitive patterns that should be varied?

Figure 4–2. Basic questions about style that writers should ask about their writing.

"introduction." Since style is the basic element in the writer-audience interaction, nothing is so illustrative of style as the introduction—which has often been likened to the label on a can, something which not only "names" the contents but attracts the "buyer" as well. But the writing of professional nurses is so very diversified that it is difficult to make generalizations about the introduction. A research report or grant application may require a synopsis of the entire project as the introduction, whereas a journal may (or may not, depending on the particular journal) require a "catchy" opener, and in the business letter still another style of opening is called for. We have, therefore, reserved "introductions" as elements of the specific types of writing discussed in Part II—Process in Practice.

EXERCISES

I. Combine each of the following groups of sentences to avoid *wordiness:*

    A. Clients who are poorly educated are difficult to instruct about health care.

They do not have the background of human anatomy and physiology to understand many basic concepts.

The nurse-educator must be patient.

B. Biofeedback is a technique for stress management.

Equipment is used to give the client information about physiological processes.

Biofeedback is a relatively new technique.

C. Nutrition education is important for weight control.

Many obese clients are actually malnourished.

Many obese clients have poor eating habits.

II. Compare *your* styles:

A. Write a letter to your best friend about nursing as a profession.

B. Write an article (500 words) for a local newspaper about nursing as a profession.

C. Compare and contrast your "style" in A and B.

III. Using the checklist in Figure 4-2, analyze your style from any sample of writing you've done recently. Write a one paragraph description of the style you observe.

PART II

PROCESS IN PRACTICE

CHAPTER 5

Writing in the Clinical Care Setting

WHAT'S WRITTEN AND WHY

In previous chapters we have shown the importance of written communication in the implementation of the nursing process. This chapter will focus on the writing required in the clinical setting. Although specific writing requirements will vary from setting to setting (e.g., different types of forms, documentation procedures) and with different clinical responsibilities, the writing *process*, just as the nursing process, remains unchanged.

Clinical care settings vary dramatically—from the ICU where nurses chart continuously, to the nursing home where charting is done perhaps only on a weekly basis. And nurses' documentation in community agencies or health departments will again be different. Just as nurses master the nursing process so that they may care effectively in a variety of settings and meet the varied needs of many different clients, so too must they master the writing process to be able to communicate health care information clearly, concisely, and accurately regardless of the clinical care setting.

The Hospital

In the hospital setting patient care is the responsibility of a team of health care professionals, and the written transmission of information among them:

- Provides continuity of care

- Prevents duplication of efforts
- Reduces the chance of error or omission
- Results in a record of the type and quality of care given

The nurse's role in recording and documenting information reflects the changes in the nursing profession over the past generation. Fifty years ago nurses did not record observations; they routinely initialed a completed activity. Ten years ago it was principally the head nurse who wrote the patient's care plan. Today every R.N. in a clinical care setting routinely records observations and writes orders for ancillary personnel. Nurses do not merely employ their own knowledge, skill, and education in direct patient care; they record and document for other health care professionals to extend their care through others. Transmission of information is of major importance in the nursing process.

The principal writing responsibilities of the nurse in a clinical care setting are:

- **Nursing Care Plan**
- **Patient Chart**

Among the members of the health care team, it is the nurse who is specifically responsible for assisting the patient with ongoing, daily personal health care maintenance as well as with any needs arising from the illness or reason for hospitalization. This is accomplished by initiating the nursing process with a comprehensive patient assessment, followed by the development of an individualized plan of care, the Nursing Care Plan. It is true that the physician is responsible for the medical diagnosis and treatment and will write medical orders for the nurse and other team members to follow, but such medical orders represent only one facet of interventions necessary for total patient care. Implementing these medical orders *is* a primary responsibility of the nurse, but it is also true that by *only* implementing these medical orders, nurses will be giving fragmented rather than holistic care. The specific responsibility of the nurse is to do a thorough assessment and formulate a **written** care plan for the patient.

Nurses in the clinical setting are more attuned to intervention than detailed written planning, yet both are vital to the overall care of the patient. It is important to recognize the reality of the clinical situation. The parent caring for a sick child at home or the adult caring for an elderly parent has a minimal need to systematize that care, but in any modern health care facility systematic methods are needed to organize and manage patient care information. The Nursing Care Plan represents one of the major writing responsibilities of the nurse.

Care planning has always been an integral part of nursing, though the plan may have been more informal in the past. Today, federal and state governing and review agencies have made the Nursing Care Plan a basic requirement for evaluation of nursing quality. Care planning has become a universal requirement for licensing and accreditation of nursing service agencies. Yet many professional nurses are resistant to this regulation and resent the time spent "writing" when they feel they could be employing their skills more usefully. One hospital we are familiar with has developed preprinted care plans, individual plans written for every conceivable diagnosis, so that the nurse need only date and initial actions rather than plan and record them. The change to the preprinted forms was directly caused by their nurses' reluctance to write care plans.

One reason for this resistance to care planning among nurses is the confusion that exists about care plans. It is important to note that there are two styles of nursing care planning related to function. As a student your care plan will be primarily for educational purposes, whereas the staff nurse's care plan should be specifically designed for service delivery. The student's plan must be comprehensive and exhaustive (*exhausting,* students claim) so that the instructor can evaluate the student's ability to assess and plan effectively. Students' care plans facilitate their grasp of the problem-solving process as it applies to nursing and should also include scientific principles and rationale. A nursing education care plan should include the following elements:

1. Documentation of client data from assessment
2. Identification and definition of client's problems
3. Statement of the scientific facts and principles relating to the problem, including its cause

4. Statement of the expected outcomes or objectives, including deadlines and checking intervals
5. List of the specific nursing actions that are designed to solve the problem
6. Rationale and scientific principles that justify the recommended care
7. Description of the client's responses to care
8. Evaluation of the success or failure of the recommended nursing actions by analyzing the client's response
9. Recommendations pertaining to maintaining or revising the nursing actions

A carefully written plan will improve the student's critical thinking skills, enabling the student to internalize the care planning procedures so that they can be done mentally and informally where necessary—in the Emergency Department, for example, where the care must often be planned and carried out before there is time for writing the plan. It is the memory of these detailed student care plans, however, that seems to evoke such reluctance to care plans among professional nurses.

The staff nurse's care plan, though, is not like the student's. It should be *specifically designed for service delivery*. Its primary purpose should be to communicate relevant data rapidly and efficiently to other team members regarding the required strategies for patient care. The dramatic difference between a *student's* educational care plan and one written by a staff nurse for care delivery is illustrated in Figures 5-1 and 5-2. After assessing the patient, a 71-year-old male with the medical diagnosis of inguinal hernia, the student identified 16 problems, possible and actual, and wrote a thorough plan according to the educational model. Figure 5-1 illustrates only the first three problems as detailed by the student. Figure 5-2 illustrates how those three problems have been reduced to two by a nurse writing the care plan in the clinical setting and shows how much more concise and specific the care plan is when designed for service delivery. While the student care plan is designed to improve the student's understanding of the nursing process, the R.N.'s care plan is designed to facilitate the nursing process.

Problems	Expected Outcomes	Actions	Rationale with Footnotes	Evaluation
Possible problem of respiratory depression due to muscle depression after surgery	Pt. will not develop respiratory depression as evident by no signs of hypoxia which are slow, shallow respirations, nail bed cyanosis, restlessness, nor pulse, during post-op hospitalization	1 assess respirations q 4 hr 2 cough and deep breathe q x 2 hr 3 assess pulse q 4 hr 4 assess nail beds for cyanosis q 2 hr	Respiratory problems may develop during first 48 hr post-op; it is necessary to assess respiratory functions to be on guard for hypoxia to prevent uncomfortable procedures for the patient, C & DB will promote better respiratory fx by clearing mucus and increasing lung expansion.	Goal Met—pt. did not develop respiratory depression; respirations were normal—20 breaths/min, no cyanosis of nail beds, pulse 90 beats/min., no signs of restlessness
Possible problem of pneumonia and atelectasis due to immobility and anesthesia	Pt. will not develop pneumonia nor atelectasis as evidenced by no signs of tachycardia, no elevated temperature, no thick greenish, pulent, foul-	1 Assess temp q 4 hr 2 Assess pulse q 4 hr 3 Position pt. correctly on side to encourage draining	Skilled nursing care can help prevent some pneumonias, thus by implementing these nursing actions the pt. will not develop pneumonia nor atelactasis; e.g..	Goal Met—pt. did not develop pneumonia nor atelactasis; no tachycardia; no temp., sputum was clear, white and thick then thin with

Figure 5-1. A Care Plan prepared by a nursing student for a nursing instructor. (Compare Fig. 5-2.)

Problems	Expected Outcomes	Actions	Rationale with Footnotes	Evaluation
	smelling sputum, during post-op hospitalization	4 Encourage coughing and deep breathing 5 x q 2 hr 5 Administer O$_2$ as necessary 6 Encourage pt. to turn q 2 hr 7 Promote well balanced diet at all meals and snacks 8 CPT prn 9 Ambulate as ordered	turning prevents accumulation of secretion in lungs; coughing helps remove potentially infectious secretions; a well balanced diet will help cause production of plasma cells lost during illness and O$_2$ will aid c dyspnea.	no odor Pulse = 90 beat/min Temp = 37
Potential problem of hemorrhage due to surgery	Pt. will not develop hemorrhage as evidenced by no blood at site of incision, no B.P., no pulse, No pallor nor coldness during post-op hospitalization	1 Assess BP, pulse q 2 hr 2 Assess nail beds and temperature of skin 3 Assess dressing q 2 hr 4 Advise pt to report any bloody discharge or dark colored	Hemorrhage is a major complication post-op and should be watched for carefully since excessive blood loss can result in quick death; due to blood loss the BP will drop as will the pulse; reduced blood flow will cause skin to	Goal Met—pt. did not develop hemorrhage; no pallor nor coldness and there was no blood at site of incision. BP 122/80 Pulse 90

discharge from
incision areas as
well as any
throbbing or
pain in the
incision area

5 If occurs, notify
doctor, apply
pressure to site
and stay with pt.,
reassuring him

become cold and
cyanotic in extremities
first; also blood will be
visible.

Figure 5-1. (Continued)

Problem	Expected Outcome	Nursing Actions
Atelectasis and hypostatic pneumonia (possible)	No respiratory problems, chest clear	1 Turn, cough, and deep breathe q 2 hr on even hr 2 Breath sounds, pulse, B.P. T q 4 hr 3 Inspirometic T.I.D. 10, 2, 6 4 Encourage movement in bed 5 Ambulate as ordered
Post-op hemorrhage (possible)	No excessive blood loss	1 Vitals 1 ½ hr x 4, then q 1 hr until stable, then q 4 hr 2 Check dressing

Figure 5-2. A Care Plan for same client as in Figure 5-1, prepared by an RN in a clinical setting.

Students must understand how the care plan functions in actual practice. You may have a patient with a feeding tube and write the nursing action:

Irrigate feeding tube p.r.n.

Your nursing order will serve any other qualified caregiver, so that if the feeding tube must be irrigated at 11 PM, and you have worked the 7-3 shift, another nurse will perform the necessary nursing action. You have insured continuity of care for your patient. Clearly, the nursing plan does not include *all* possible situations. Suppose the feeding tube becomes blocked, and a nurse who is unfamiliar with the care of a patient with a feeding tube has just been assigned to the patient and does not know how to proceed. The instructions are *not* expected to be in the care plan. The nurse would naturally ask for assistance from the team leader or another team member familiar with the procedure. The care plan is not designed to be the *only* communication among members of a health care team, but anyone who has ever experienced the distortions to which oral communication is susceptible (ever play the game "Gossip" as a child?) understands why basic nursing care needs a reliable, verifiable, and systematic procedure for transmitting information. The Nursing Care Plan fulfills this need, and that is why it has become such a universal requirement for licensing and accreditation of nursing service agencies.

More comprehensive than the **Nursing Care Plan** is the **patient's chart,** which is the individual's health care record. The form of the chart, like the form for the care plan, will vary from agency to agency, unit to unit, but typically the chart includes:

- Record of admission
- Personal data sheet
- Consent forms
- Nursing history
- Medical history
- Physical examination findings
- Progress sheets
- Laboratory and procedure date sheets

- Flow sheets
- Physician's orders
- Medication record
- Discharge planning record
- Utilization review sheet

There are two different approaches to recording that every professional nurse should be familiar with:

1. **Traditional** *(also known as source-oriented): In this type of recording, each health care professional functions according to a role, so the chart is composed of separate sections for each group. For example, physicians record their evaluations under "Physician's Progress Notes," while nurses record their observations in a separate section of "Nurses' Notes."*

2. **Problem-Oriented Record (POR):** *Dr. Lawrence L. Weed developed this problem-oriented record-keeping system in the late sixties. It is an orderly system of charting designed to communicate in writing the process of patient care. The problem-oriented record has four components:*

   1. *A data base*
   2. *An analysis of the data base (list of problems)*
   3. *A plan (for treatment of problems)*
   4. *Report on treatments (progress notes)*

In this system, charting is done according to the problems presented by the client, and the health care professionals integrate their observations and evaluations in relation to the problem, regardless of the specific role of the team member. And so both the nursing history and physical examination findings would be included in "Data Base," and both physician's progress notes and nurse's notes would be in the final section, "Report on Treatments." These progress notes also reflect the problem-oriented approach as they are written to include:

- *Subjective data*
- *Objective data*

- *Assessment*
- *Plan*

The POR format is usually referred to by the acronym SOAP. Figure 5-3 illustrates the differences in progress notes between the traditional and POR forms for a patient with depression.

The emergence of the problem-oriented record reflects a definite trend in the health care system, an emphasis on the client and on the problem-solving approach in fostering the client's well-being. This record-keeping system stresses complementarity among team members regardless of specific responsibilities on the team. For the nurse, this type of recording makes the nursing process more visible.

Whether you use traditional or POR forms of recording will depend on the agency in which you practice. Just as student nurses write care plans according to the format assigned by the instructor, R.N.s document according to the system used by their agency. But what both the students and the R.N.s need to know are the basic principles of recording that are common to all settings. The forms you will use are not permanent; the skills are.

Progress Notes	
Traditional (Patient with medical diagnosis of depression)	**P.O.R.**
7 AM Pt. c/o fatigue—states "Didn't sleep at all last night." Did not eat breakfast. Flat affect.	Problem #1 Depression
	S—no appetite; unable to sleep
	O—flat affect; ate no breakfast; pacing in hallway
7:30 AM Pacing in hall—refuses to join group therapy.	A—continuing to exhibit signs of clinical depression
	P—continue Elavil B.I.D.; encourage to join group therapy

Figure 5–3. Progress notes in traditional and POR form.

HOW IT'S WRITTEN

Recording, the basic writing task of the nurse in a clinical care setting, seems to have a language all its own. The beginning nursing student who tries to read the order

O.O.B. for 1/2° B.I.D.

might be bewildered, but this is simply a clear, concise statement that the patient is to be gotten out of bed for half an hour twice a day. The first time students see this type of order, they might assume that the abbreviations and specialized vocabulary make recording extremely difficult. But most students absorb this "new language" easily with the aid of a list of approved abbreviations and preferred terms.

Unfortunately, there is little actual instruction in principles of recording, and most students learn simply from imitating the charting notes they observe in their clinical practice. Effective recording requires not simply a knowledge of proper abbreviations but an understanding of the principles of documentation— **objectivity, precision** and **completeness.**

To understand more fully, let's look again at the basic writer's triangle (Fig. 5-4).

In recording, the subject (care delivery) can never be separated from the sense of audience (other health care professionals). Information is recorded principally so that it can be read by others, and that underlying dynamic pervades all discussion of technique in documentation. Since communication is the underlying premise behind all recording, entries must be objective, precise, and complete. Attention to all three aspects of clinical documentation is the hallmark of the truly professional nurse.

Objective Recording

Nursing students are schooled in objective assessment, so this principle is usually followed. Objective recording means that the nurse is limited to "What I know and how I know it." Objective recording means that the nurse will *not* write a note:

NURSE/WRITER

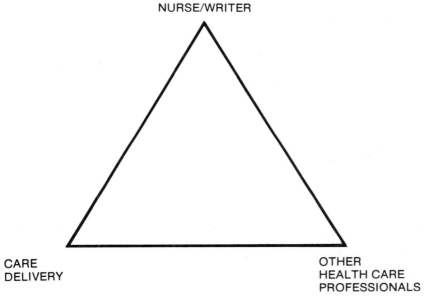

CARE
DELIVERY

OTHER
HEALTH CARE
PROFESSIONALS

Figure 5–4. The basic dynamic of the writing process for the nurse as writer.

   3 PM   Pt. is anxious about impending surgery

but will record the patient's anxiety with attention to data:

   3 PM   Pt. questioned nurse about impending surgery 4x since
              11 AM admission—tense facial expression—did not eat
              lunch

Note: Objective recording should not be confused with objective
data. As POR makes clear, data may be both objective (observable)
or subjective (symptoms as given by the patient).

    It is important for both medical and legal reasons that the
record be free of judgmental statements. The comment

   7 PM   Pt. complained about order to change positions q 2 hr

is not helpful to other members of the team. Did the patient actually change positions in spite of the complaining? A more *objective* note would be:

7 PM   Pt. refused to change position 3 PM and 5 PM

The latter note gives needed information to other members of the health care team and protects the nurse against any charge of failure to carry out the order to change positions.

Precise Recording
To write accurate, clear notes in a concise way involves the use of specialized vocabulary and abbreviations with attention to sentence structure, punctuation, spelling, and handwriting.

Abbreviations. The use of abbreviations enables the nurse to record accurately, completely, and quickly. In order to be effective, the use of abbreviations must be consistent throughout any particular agency. The American Hospital Association publishes a list of acceptable initials and abbreviations. Unfortunately, not all agencies limit themselves to the abbreviations on this list. Most, in fact, orient nurses with their own list of "authorized medical abbreviations." Very often you will find that such lists are a combination of standard medical abbreviations, standard pharmacological abbreviations, and idiosyncratic abbreviations which are in use in that particular agency. Figure 5–5 illustrates the "A" section of one hospital's abbreviation list. The items printed in boldface are also found on the American Hospital Association's list of accepted abbreviations; the items italicized are standard pharmacological abbreviations; all the others appear to be idiosyncratic to this particular agency.

As a professional nurse, you will be responsible for adapting to the procedures of the agency for which you work. Thus, if you have been regularly using the abbreviation "s.o.s." on your current placement and find that it is *not* used in the next agency in which you work, you should not use "s.o.s" in that setting *even though it is accepted as standard by the American Hospital Association.* As we stated earlier, in order to be effective, the use of abbreviations must be consistent throughout any particular agency. So you also cannot

Abbreviation	Definition
A	apical (pulse)
@	at
aa	*of each*
AA&O	awake, alert & oriented
abd. or abdom	**abdomen**
ABG	arterial blood gases
A.C.	acromial clavicular
a.c.	**before meals**
ad	*to; up to*
ad lib	*at pleasure; as much as needed*
ADL	activities of daily living
adm	admit; admitted
A.D.P.L.	average daily patient load
adv	against
A.F.B.	acid fast bacillus
A.J.	ankle jerks
A.K.	above knee
alveol	alveoloplasty
A.M.	morning; before noon
Amp	ampere
Angio	angiocath
ant	anterior
ante ....,....	before
AP	antepartum
A&P	anterior and posterior
APR	anterior posterior resection
AROM	artificial rupture of membranes
art	arterial
ASCVD	Arteriosclerotic cardiovascular
	disease
A.S.H.D.	Arteriosclerotic heart disease
aq	*water*
ax	axilla
A.U.	both ears

Figure 5-5. Sample page of one hospital's list of accepted abbreviations.

include your own personal abbreviations. You may have begun using shortened versions of frequently used words in your own class notes, for example, but unless *drsg.* is accepted for *dressing* throughout the agency in which you work, you should not use your own shortened version of the word. Accepted abbreviations vary from agency to agency, and part of your professional responsibility is to familiarize yourself with the accepted abbreviations of your agency and use only those in its records.

Specialized Vocabulary. Student nurses usually acquire their medical vocabularly gradually in the course of their education and clinical experience. Students learn the preferred descriptive terms from textbooks and instructors and soon learn to observe "distended abdomen" rather than "swollen belly" and "dyspnea" instead of "difficult breathing." The student who feels the need of increased attention to medical vocabulary might refer to *A Handbook and Charting Manual for Student Nurses* by Alice L. Price (Mosby, 1971 [especially pp. 196–208], which lists the commonly used medical descriptive terms. Keep in mind, however, that keeping your clinical vocabularly up-to-date will be a life-long professional responsibility. Such journal features as *R.N.*'s monthly "Check you Clinical Wordpower" provide regular assessments for nurses.

Sentence Structure and Punctuation. Charting entries are most often notes and not usually written in complete sentences. This means that the group of words does not have the "standard" structure that communicates in our language, and the nurse must be sure that the fragment communicates the thought effectively. Since the usual subject of the note is "Pt," the basic structure is verb-complement:

Example:

Nursing Care Plan	Patient Chart
1. Orient to surroundings	Oriented to surroundings
2. Keep foot elevated to reduce edema	Head of bed elevated

3. Assess and administer pain 2 PM—c/o sharp,
meds as needed stabbing pain in L foot;
Demerol, 150 mg I.M. in
R gluteus.

In the care plan, orders are usually written on separate lines (as above), but when reporting symptoms (as in the final charting note about pain), items are often listed in series, and it is important to separate them effectively. Both the semicolon and the dash are strong and effective dividers.

Example:

c/o visual disturbance; headache; polyuria—skin dry and flushed

or

Alert but drowsy; easily awakened; left arm immobilized

or

Turn from back to left side q 2 hr when awake—elevate arm 30° when on side

Note that the entry is *punctuated for intonation;* i.e, the choice of punctuation is determined by what the nurse is trying to communicate. Always write *thoughts,* not just words, when you are charting. You want your reader to *see* as you do.

Spelling. In Chapter 2 we emphasized the importance of correct spelling for the nurse's professional image. The same is true in recording. Ironically, nurses are usually accurate with the difficult technical terms they must master, like "diaphoresis" and "presbyopia" but can fail with the more common health-related words like "hemorrhage" or "immunization." The advice in Chapter 2 pertains here as well; master the words required in your professional writing with the care you would take to master any skill required of you as a nurse.

A more serious area of concern in charting is not misspelling but a widespread tendency to leave off word suffixes. So the note

> Demerol 200 mg administer 2 PM

might not only be ambiguous to other team members, but it could be challenged in a court of law since "administer" does not mean the same thing as "administered" even if the nurse meant to write the latter word. In the same way

> Report developing congestion

does not say the same thing as

> Reported developing congestion

and while the meaning *may* be understood by other health care team members through context clues, the note may be challenged legally. If you know that you have this tendency in your writing (and it is *very* common), you must try to correct the problem. When you are charting quickly in a care giving situation, your writing reflexes have to be accurate.

Handwriting. It may seem obvious, but it is important to remember that the Nursing Care Plan and patient's chart are specifically written to be read by others, so legible handwriting is not an option; it is part of your professional responsibility. Should you expect another team member to read *diaphoretic* as *diaphoretic* or to know that *edema* is *edema*? Both samples illustrate some of the more common bad habits in forming letters. In the poorly written version of *diaphoretic* there is the tendency to leave open letters that are properly closed: *u* for *a* and *v* for *o* combined with the habit of either not dotting the *i* or, as in this example, putting the dots just anywhere. This presents a real difficulty when combined with the tendency to "loop" letters like *i* and *t*. In the poorly written *edema* there is the tendency to leave open a letter which should be closed: *u* instead of *a* and the failure to close the bottom of the *d* combined with "looping" the top: this *cl* rather than *d*. Bad habits in forming letters can be corrected with a little attention and care. It is a mark of professional courtesy to make sure that other team members will be able to decipher your handwriting. And since the patient's chart is also a legal record, it is prudent to write legibly.

Another reminder regarding handwriting is that it is important that your signature is legible in all your entries. We sign our names so often in a variety of situations throughout our lives that the signature of even otherwise careful writers is very often illegible from such frequent use. But again, when patient records are legal commitments to care, the legible signature of the care giver is a professional responsibility.

Complete Recording

The first principle every student must understand is that as you develop your ability to assess your client's needs, as your professional "vision" develops, your language should reflect that development. So you may not be writing notes as completely as your instructor does right now, but you don't assess the client as thoroughly as your instructor does either. As you develop your ability to employ the nursing process more effectively, your writing should also reflect that development in the writing of more complete notes.

The complete entry is the one which says precisely what needs to be said as concisely as possible. Perhaps due to the many regulations concerning documentation (some hospitals require a minimum of one chart entry for each shift; some require charting every two hours), there is a tendency for what might be termed "non-notes" to appear on charts. Such comments as "ate well," "slept well," and "no complaints" really say nothing at all. Take, for example, "slept well." By what criteria?—Duration? Quality of sleep (lack of restlessness; no wakefulness)? Patient's comments about sleep? And there is no indication of any changes in the patient's sleeping pattern. If the fact of sleep is significant for this patient, the note might read:

> Slept 10 PM–6 AM without waking; pt. commented, "It's good to finally sleep through the night"; no request for pain med.

Note that extra words are not what makes an entry more complete; it's the presentation of data which has been collected by the nurse. By responding to their unique role as primary care givers, nurses will continually develop their assessment skills, and this will be reflected in the more complete notes written. Compare:

Poor	More Complete
2 AM c/o chest pain; physician notified	2 AM c/o dull pain(L) side of chest radiating to(L)jaw and down(L) arm; color pale; Dr. Callow notified

The poor note reflects a lack of professional awareness, a sense of the nurse as a neutral recorder of information rather than a knowledgeable professional actively involved in patient care.

Some simple rules will help you develop more complete notes:

1. Describe what you report.
It is not enough to report "Blood in stool." How much? Is it bright or dark? What are other significant characteristics of the stool?

Better:

Small amount of dark red blood on soft-formed stool, X2.

2. Avoid relative statements.
A note: "Lung congestion slightly improved" does not communicate specific information. Meaning is known only to the writer. What constitutes "improvement"?

Better:

Lungs sound clearer on auscultation and percussion. Able to expectorate tenacious mucus.

3. Give subject or time element where needed.
A care plan note to "check vital signs frequently until stable" shows very little care on the part of the writer. How often is "frequently"? Specificity *always* adds completeness.

Better:

Check vital signs on half hour until stable.

Examples:

	Poor	**More Complete**
NURSING ORDER	Turn frequently	Turn from side to side q 2 hr on even hr
CHARTING	Baby c̄ mother—nursing well	Baby nursing 5 min from each breast q 2 hr
	c/o abdominal pain	3:15 PM c/o sharp intermittent pain in RVQ. Bowel sounds present in all four quadrants—no nausea, vomiting or diarrhea
	Experiencing heavy vaginal bleeding	2:10 AM. Began heavy vaginal bleeding—bright red c̄ no clots or cramping
		3:00 AM. Bleeding remains heavy c̄ small clots—c/o cramping BP 100/70 pulse 88 Dr. Lee notified

The Community
Recording by nurses in the community setting is as varied as their roles. The community setting includes nurses who work in physicians' offices, outpatient clinics, private health care agencies, and

in private practice. In the primary care setting, the nurse's role has increased dramatically over the past 20 years and the type of recording done depends primarily on that role. Some nurses may be responsible for recording the client's presenting complaint and vital signs; others may be responsible for doing and recording an initial assessment; still others may be enacting all phases of the nursing process. Student nurses who learn to record *objectively, precisely,* and *completely* during their clinical experience will be able to practice in any primary care setting and record appropriately as required. The forms may change; the responsibilities may change; but the principles of effective recording do not.

THE REPORT

Nurses often write reports as part of their professional responsibilities. The number, frequency, and type of report will vary from agency to agency, but there are certain basic principles of report writing that remain constant. Remember that a "report" is a basic act of communication and can be either written or oral. In oral communication the receiver of the information can ask for clarification or elaboration, but the reader of a written report can rely only on the words used. That is why basic to *all* report writing is precision, clarity, coherence, and completeness.

In a general sense all we have said so far in this chapter about writing in the clinical care setting is reporting. Much of a nurse's written "reporting" is in the form of the documentation of patient care that becomes part of the chart. In discussing "the report," we are addressing principally the "incident report"—the most common type of "extraordinary" reporting for which the nurse is responsible. An *incident* is defined as any happening which is not consistent with the routine operation of the hospital or routine care of a particular client. The incident report is particularly important because it is a document used in determining liability for an accident or unusual occurrence. Most such reports are not part of the patient's chart but are for the records of the hospital attorney.

Basic to this report is a description of the incident. It is crucial that the report be accurate and objective. It is not supposed to assign blame for the incident or provide excuses for staff or express opinions. It should be complete, objective, and accurate. To write:

> Patient fell; should not have been out of bed

interprets rather than describes the incident. The more objective description:

> Patient found on floor; no apparent injury

lacks completeness, and that very lack of completeness suggests negligence regardless of how competently the nurse *actually* handled the incident. The report that reads:

> Patient Kevin Reilly found on floor next to his bed by aide, Edna Lowery, who heard call for help. Floor dry and clean. Patient was ambulating without permission; complained, "I had to pee but got dizzy." Call light was not used but was tested and found in working order. No apparent injury; physician notified.

indicates a competent and conscientious response to the incident. Remember that regardless of what actually occurred or how the situation was handled, for many concerned individuals the written report will be the only measure of the professional action taken.

Report Form

Figure 5-6 illustrates an incident report form in current use by many hospitals. Note that every effort has been made to provide guidance for the individual responsible for preparing this report by offering most of the necessary information in a checklist form. The movement toward this type of preprinted form reflects the hospital's need to insure against poor reporting. If your agency uses a more narrative form, you must be even more aware of the essential components of the incident report. From the description of Mr. Reilly's fall, we can illustrate these essential components:

Name of person involved   Kevin Reilly, patient
and designation (i.e., pa-

tient, visitor, staff, member, etc.)	
Nature of incident	Found on floor
Location of incident	Floor next to his bed
Condition of incident site	Floor dry and clean
Other person involved	Aide who heard patient call (Edna Lowery)
Circumstances	Patient was ambulating without permission
Condition of patient prior to incident	Said, "I had to pee but got dizzy."
Nature of injury	No apparent injury
Other relevant details	Call light was not used but was tested and found in working order
Physician notified?	Physician notified

The Language of Reporting

It is important to write in a clear, objective, and precise manner. Precision is important, but it is neither to assign nor to escape responsibility for the incident. Since the incident report has legal ramifications, it is professionally responsible to be as precise as possible. Precision includes clarity and completeness. There is obviously a difference between:

- Bed rails down
- Refused bed rails
- Lowered bed rails

and that difference may be vitally important. The nurse/reporter must be sure to make the necessary distinctions. Precise writing also requires specificity:

Poor: Injection error
Better: Antibiotic IM rather than IV as ordered
Poor: Wrong diet

An incident is any happening which is not consistent with the routine operation of the hospital or routine care of a particular patient. For each category mark as many items as are appropriate to adequately and completely describe the incident.

Hospital Attorney's Confidential Report of Incident (NOT PART OF MEDICAL RECORD)

FLOOR	UNIT	INCIDENT DATE	REPORT DATE	INCIDENT TIME	SHIFT
				A.M.	1st
				P.M.	2nd / 3rd

PERSON INVOLVED	SEX	AGE	DIAGNOSIS
☐ 1 - Patient ☐ 2 - Visitor ☐ 3 - Employee ☐ 4 - Volunteer	☐ 1 - F ☐ 2 - M		

No. 470352

For Patient Incidents: List Patient's Full Name or Use Addressograph Plate
For Employee and Visitor Incidents: List Full Name and Address

BRIEF DESCRIPTION OF INCIDENT; LIST WITNESSES: (Name, address, telephone - continue on reverse if necessary)

PRINT NAME AND PROFESSIONAL DESIGNATION OF PERSON COMPLETING REPORT

SUPERVISOR:

INCIDENT LOCATION

☐ 03 - CCU	☐ 21 - Laboratory	☐ 37 - Nursing-post partum	☐ 53 - Physical therapy	☐ 69 - Surgery
☐ 09 - Corridors	☐ 23 - Labor room (OB)	☐ 39 - Nursing-surgical	☐ 55 - Psychiatric unit	☐ 71 - Stairs
☐ 11 - Delivery room (OB)	☐ 24 - Laundry	☐ 41 - Occupational therapy	☐ 57 - Radiology	☐ 73 - Visitor's lounge
☐ 12 - Dietary	☐ 27 - Nuclear medicine	☐ 43 - Outpatient/clinics	☐ 59 - Recovery (Post-Anesthesia)	☐ 75 - Other ____
☐ 15 - Elevators	☐ 29 - Nursery	☐ 45 - Parking lots and sidewalks	☐ 61 - Respiratory therapy	
☐ 17 - Emergency room	☐ 31 - Nursing-medical	☐ 47 - Patient's bathroom	☐ 63 - Shower room/bathroom	
☐ 18 - ICU	☐ 33 - Nursing-orthopedic	☐ 49 - Patient's room	☐ 65 - Sitz bath	
☐ 19 - Extended care/geriatrics	☐ 35 - Nursing-pediatrics	☐ 51 - Pharmacy	☐ 67 - Special care unit	

PERSON MOST CLOSELY INVOLVED / SITE OF INJURY / CONDITION PRIOR TO INCIDENT

PERSON MOST CLOSELY INVOLVED		SITE OF INJURY		CONDITION PRIOR TO INCIDENT
☐ 04 - Aide/Orderly ☐ 20 - Pharmacist ☐ 32 - Resident		☐ 11 - Abdomen ☐ 06 - Hand		☐ 00 - Alert
☐ 08 - Graduate Nurse ☐ 22 - Pharmacy Technician ☐ 34 - Respiratory Therapist		☐ 13 - Arm(s) ☐ 01 - Head		☐ 01 - Agitated
☐ 10 - Intern ☐ 23 - Physical Therapy ☐ 36 - Student Nurse		☐ 07 - Back ☐ 15 - Leg(s)		☐ 06 - Disoriented/confused
☐ 12 - I.V. Nurse ☐ 24 - Physician ☐ 38 - Technician/Technologist		☐ 14 - Buttocks ☐ 05 - Neck		☐ 13 - Paralysis
☐ 14 - Licensed Practical Nurse ☐ 26 - Psychiatric Technician ☐ 39 - Volunteer		☐ 09 - Chest ☐ 17 - None or NA		☐ 22 - Sedated
☐ 16 - Nurse Anesthetist (CRNA) ☐ 28 - Psychiatric Therapist ☐ 40 - Other - ____		☐ 03 - Face ☐ 10 - Toe(s)		☐ 26 - Uncooperative
☐ 18 - Nurse and Pharmacist ☐ 30 - Registered Nurse		☐ 12 - Finger(s) ☐ 18 - Other - ____		☐ 29 - Weak/Faint/Dizzy
		☐ 08 - Foot		☐ 31 - Other - ____

INCIDENT TYPE - MEDICATION / INCIDENT TYPE - FALLS

INCIDENT TYPE - MEDICATION		INCIDENT TYPE - FALLS	
☐ 18 - Administered without order ☐ 30 - Medication theft/missing ☐ 44 - Wrong rate		☐ 01 - Ambulating/with permission ☐ 13 - Incontinent	
☐ 20 - Adverse medication reaction ☐ 32 - Omission ☐ 46 - Wrong route		☐ 02 - Ambulating/without permission ☐ 17 - Lost Balance/Dizzy	
☐ 22 - After discontinued ☐ 38 - Transfusion error ☐ 47 - Wrong site		☐ 03 - Bed-rails up/restrained ☐ 18 - Lowered side rail(s)	
☐ 24 - Duplication ☐ 40 - Wrong dose ☐ 48 - Wrong time		☐ 04 - Bed-rails up/no restraints ☐ 19 - Refused restraints	
☐ 26 - I.V. Infiltration ☐ 42 - Wrong medication ☐ 50 - Other - ____		☐ 06 - Bed-rails down/restrained ☐ 21 - Refused side rails	
☐ 28 - Medication on hold		☐ 08 - Bed-rails down/no restraints ☐ 23 - Removed restraint(s)	

MEDICATION INVOLVED

☐ 02 - Analgesic	☐ 14 - Antihistamine	☐ 26 - Steroid
☐ 04 - Antiarrhythmic	☐ 18 - Diuretic	☐ 28 - Unmedicated I.V.Solution
☐ 06 - Anticoagulant	☐ 21 - Laxative	☐ 30 - Vasodilator
☐ 08 - Anticonvulsant	☐ 22 - Narcotic	☐ 32 - Vasopressor
☐ 10 - Antidepressant	☐ 24 - Sedative/Tranquilizer	☐ 34 - Other - ____

(falls continued)
☐ 05 - Call light not used ☐ 29 - Unable to follow instructions
☐ 10 - Chair or equipment/restrained ☐ 33 - Violated activity order
☐ 12 - Chair or equipment/no restraints ☐ 71 - Visitor assisted Pt. in ambulating
☐ 11 - Fainted   without staff assistance
☐ 35 - Found on floor ☐ 81 - Other - ____
☐ 07 - Improper footwear

DESCRIPTION OF MEDICATION INCIDENT / INCIDENT TYPE - OTHER

DESCRIPTION OF MEDICATION INCIDENT		INCIDENT TYPE - OTHER	
☐ 02 - Container contents not checked	☐ 44 - Patient not observed until medication (oral) was taken	☐ 52 - Assaults	☐ 86 - Patient escape
☐ 04 - Container improperly labeled	☐ 48 - Patient's allergies not checked	☐ 56 - Broken/malfunctioning equipment	☐ 87 - Smoking
☐ 06 - Container label not checked	☐ 50 - Patient's I.D. band not checked	☐ 58 - Caught In/On/Between	☐ 88 - Struck against
☐ 10 - Direct copy of physician's order not checked	☐ 58 - Route of administration not checked	☐ 60 - Contact with heat	☐ 90 - Struck by
☐ 14 - Blood crossmatching/typing	☐ 60 - Time lapse since last dosage not verified	☐ 62 - Diagnostic test at wrong time/sequence	☐ 92 - Surgery check list not completed
☐ 22 - Incorrect calculation of dosage	☐ 62 - Transcription error	☐ 64 - Needle stick	☐ 94 - Wrong diet
☐ 26 - I.V not monitored	☐ 64 - Unclear order not reviewed with physician	☐ 66 - Fire	☐ 95 - Wrong treatment/diagnostic test
☐ 28 - Med. card not compared with unit med. profile/Kardex	☐ 66 - Unit med. profile/Kardex not checked frequently as reminder	☐ 71 - Consent	☐ 96 - Other - ____
☐ 30 - Med. cup not compared with med. card	☐ 68 - Unit med. profile/Kardex not compared with direct copy of physician's order	☐ 72 - Lost/damaged Pt./Visitor property	
☐ 34 - Med./IV placed in wrong location (shelf, unit dose tray, etc.)	☐ 72 - Wrong dosage or strength from pharmacy	☐ 74 - Lost specimens	
☐ 40 - Patient drug profile not kept up-to-date and accurate on unit	☐ 74 - Wrong IV equipment used	☐ 76 - Missing instrument(s)	WAS PHYSICIAN NOTIFIED?
	☐ 76 - Wrong med. from pharmacy	☐ 78 - Missing needle(s)	☐ YES ☐ NO
	☐ 78 - Other -	☐ 80 - Missing sponge(s)	TIME NOTIFIED ____ A.M.
		☐ 82 - Omitted diagnostic test	____ P.M.
		☐ 84 - Omitted treatment	

NATURE OF INJURY

☐ 01 - Abrasion	☐ 11 - Back	☐ 23 - Deceased	☐ 45 - Puncture	☐ 41 - No Apparent Injury
☐ 03 - Aggravation of pre-existing condition	☐ 15 - Broken tooth/teeth	☐ 25 - Fracture - Dislocation	☐ 47 - Sprain/strain	☐ 51 - Not Applicable
☐ 05 - Allergic Reaction	☐ 17 - Burns	☐ 27 - Head Injury	☐ 50 - X-Ray ordered	☐ 49 - Other - ____
	☐ 21 - Contusion	☐ 37 - Laceration		

PHYSICIAN'S STATEMENT

PRINT PHYSICIAN'S NAME

HOSPITAL COPY - USE REVERSE SIDE IF NECESSARY   OHIC 10/80

Figure 5–6. Sample incident report form.

Better: Regular menu received and eaten rather than diabetic diet ordered

Qualifying words often seep into the incident report and should be avoided. The greatest offenders are *may, seems, possibly, might, appears, apparently.*

> *Not this:* Patient apparently fell
> *This:*   Patient found on floor

There is no need to speculate about what happened. You are to describe what was observed.

> *Not this:* Call light may have malfunctioned
> *This:*   Call light checked; was operative

Yes, it may *have malfunctioned; but you are only to report what is observable and verifiable.*

> *Not this:* Speciment possibly lost
> *This:*   Speciment lost

Of course, there's always the possibility that it may turn up somewhere, but if the purpose of the report is to document the incident, and if the incident concerns the fact that the specimen cannot be located, then regardless of where it may be, the specimen is lost.

ASSESSMENT

Assessment is that stage of the nursing process designed to gather data to provide a foundation on which to build nursing diagnoses, plans, interventions, and evaluations that will facilitate wellness in the client. The skills associated with assessment are usually regarded as oral communication (taking the health history) or clinical technique (performing the physical examination). Yet, since the purpose of assessment is to provide the foundation for the effective implementation of the nursing process, the assessment is *recorded.* And although there are many skills required for an effective clinical assessment, skill in written communication should not be overlooked. When the nurse leaves the client, it is the *recorded* findings that represent that client, both physically and psychosocially, to both the nurse and other health care professionals. That is why it is essential for the nurse to understand the *written* aspects of assessment.

In assessment, interviewing and recording skills interface. For example, if the nurse elicits a vague response from the client and accepts and records that response, the problem may be with the nurse's interviewing skills, but a poorly written assessment is the result. So in assessment all the nursing skills are interdependent, and the nurse must acquire and develop a holistic approach to assessment, understanding that not only good listening skills are needed, but also good skills in observing, interviewing, recording, etc. Since the *written* assessment is the product of the assessment process, we will discuss the entire process as it relates to the writing task involved. As with all writing tasks, we can understand the nature of assessment as writing by looking at our basic writer's triangle (Fig. 5-7).

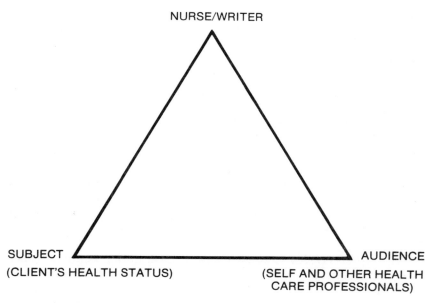

Figure 5-7. The basic dynamic of the writing process for the nurse as writer.

What Is the Task?

In the particular "writing task" known as assessment, the nurse selects, organizes, and analyzes data relevant to the subject (client's health status) at this particular time and records that data for self and other health care professionals (audience). As we look at assessment from the perspective of a writing task, it is clear that the objective is to present the subject (client's health status) to the audience (health care professionals) in order to effect positive change in the client's health. As in all writing tasks, a knowledge of the dynamic between writer (nurse), subject (client's health status), and audience (self and other health care professionls) helps focus the nurse's attention on the essential aspects of the task.

What Are the Components of the Task?

Client assessment includes a *health history, physical findings,* and *laboratory data.* Many aspects of the physical examination and laboratory data are directly relevant to clinical skills. Taking the health history, however, is not only the most important element of the assessment since it serves to direct the examiner in the physical exam, but it is also the portion of the assessment that is most dependent on the nurse's communication skills—both oral and written.

The assessment also includes both subjective and objective data, and it is important for the nurse to distinguish between them in writing and recording the assessment. The client offers *symptoms* (subjective data); the examiner identifies *signs* (objective data) during the physical exam, or from laboratory findings. For example, a client may complain of a sore throat and difficulty in swallowing (symptoms), while the physical examination may reveal a cherry red exudative pharynx, an elevated temperature, and swollen glands (signs), and the subsequent throat culture may reveal a strep infection (sign). Taking the health history is primarily the eliciting of symptoms, the subjective data.

The Health History. Regardless of the situation being assessed, the nurse collects information in a variety of specific areas. Figure 5-8 illustrates a typical worksheet for the client history. It is important to note that "taking a history" does not mean simply recording the information offered by the client, but also interviewing both the

NAME _____

ADDRESS _____

AGE _____ **SEX** _____ **MARITAL STATUS** _____

RACE _____ **RELIGION** _____

OCCUPATION _____

USUAL SOURCE OF MEDICAL CARE _____

SOURCE AND RELIABILITY OF INFORMATION _____

CHIEF COMPLAINT:

PRESENT ILLNESS:

PAST HISTORY:
Childhood Illnesses:

Immunizations:

Allergies:

Hospitalizations and Serious Illnesses:

Figure 5–8. Sample of a typical worksheet for client history. _(From Block N D: Heath Assessment for Professional Nursing New York, Appleton-Century-Crofts, 1981, pp 37-41. Reprinted with permission.)_

Accidents:

Obstetrics History:

Medications:

Habits:

*Prenatal History:**

*Labor and Delivery History:**

*Neonatal History:**

REVIEW OF SYSTEMS:
General:

Skin:

Hair:

*Recorded for a child under 4 years of age with cogenital or developmental problems.
Figure 5-8. (Continued)

Nails:

Head:

Eyes:

Ears:

Nose and Sinuses:

Oral Cavity:

Neck:

Nodes:

Breast:

Respiratory:

Figure 5-8. (Continued)

133

Cardiovascular:

Gastrointestinal:

Genitourinary:

Menstrual History:

Back:

Extremities:

Neurologic:

Hematopoietic:

Endocrine:

FAMILY HISTORY:

Figure 5-8. (Continued)

NUTRITIONAL HISTORY:

SOCIAL DATA:
Family Relationships and Friendships:

Ethnic Affiliation:

Occupational History:

Educational History:

Economic Status:

Living Circumstances:

Pattern of Health Care:

DEVELOPMENTAL HISTORY:

Figure 5-8. (Continued)

SEXUAL HISTORY:

PATIENT'S ACTIVITY TO REMAIN HEALTHY:

Figure 5–8. (Continued)

client and his or her family, noting nonverbal communications and inferences drawn from the observation of behavior. The *recorded* history is a synthesis and is intended to give the reader a clear picture of the client and his or her health situation.

Approach to Taking the History. The nurse is not merely a channel through which information flows—ear to pen on paper— instead, the nurse is a health care professional who must organize and analyze the raw data (subjective and objective information received), making inferences about their meaning and relationship to the individual's health state. Taking a health history is a complex task requiring many communication skills.

Since the amount of information required is so vast, a predetermined format should be used during the interview (see Fig. 5-8), but the nurse must understand that this form is merely a guideline to help make sure that all areas of the individual's health status are considered. It should not be used as a checklist or series of questions. The nurse's knowledge and experience must determine the individual questions for each client and situation. The nurse's attitude should not be one of simply gathering information impersonally; he or she should establish rapport with the client. The nurse must communicate openness and caring. The aim should be to have a friendly conversation with the client, a conversation which is focused on eliciting factors relevant to the client's current health status. Obviously notes will have to be taken because of the sheer volume of information elicited. However, the emphasis should be on relating to the client, so the nurse should make every effort to write minimally and maintain eye contact with the client. Only notes are taken; the actual history is written after the assessment has been completed.

Techniques of Taking the History
Listening. The center of the health history is allowing the client to tell his or her own story. During this time, not only can the nurse/interviewer learn a great deal of factual information, but he or she can also assess the client's emotional status, personality, and level of intellectual functioning. The nurse's attentive, nonjudgmental attitude in listening establishes a level of trust with the client. Obviously, the nurse/interviewer will need to take notes while listening, but this must be done as unobtrusively as possible.

Questioning. From listening to the client's story and observing the nonverbal cues as well, the nurse asks relevant questions to clarify or add to what has been offered. There is no set list of questions to be considered; the nurse responds professionally to the client as indicated by the situation. However, there are some important caveats:

1. It is preferable to use the open-ended approach whenever possible:

"Tell me about the pain in your ankle."

is preferable to:

"Does your ankle only hurt when you walk?"

The latter question might elicit simply a positive or negative response, while the first question encourages the client to verbalize and, therefore, give a more complete answer which will, in turn, be more helpful to the nurse/interviewer.

2. Avoid leading questions. Don't say

"Your ankle doesn't hurt when you're sitting does it?"

Such leading questions indicate the response expected (in this case, "No") and can intimidate the client who may hesitate to offer a response other than the one obviously expected.

3. Offer help when necessary. *Even the open-ended request,*

"Describe your pain."

may be a problem to the client who is unaware how *to describe pain. (To most nonprofessionals all pain simply "hurts.") It may be more helpful in such cases to offer the client choices:*

"How would you describe your pain?—sharp? dull and aching? throbbing?"

(Don't lapse into leading questions in such situations. To ask,

"Is it a sharp pain?"

may confuse the client who thinks the severity of the pain is being questioned.)

4. Avoid technical language as much as possible. *Obviously, the nurse would try to use language that is familiar to the client.*

Asking,

"Do you have trouble urinating?"

is preferable to asking,

"Do you have trouble voiding?"

The nurse should also be aware of the fact that there are many common words and phrases that have different connotations in health care. For example, avoid saying:

"I understand that you've been complaining about pain in your ankle."

Although this indeed may be the client's "chief complaint" at the moment, he or she may interpret your statement as a criticism, since the common understanding of the word complaining *is to express discontent. It's better to alter your habitual use of the word and say.*

"I understand that you've been having pain in your ankle."

Observing. Although usually associated with the physical examination, observation begins during the history with the nurse/interviewer, who is aware of factors that may relate to the presenting problem. During this interview the nurse should be conscious of noting the client's general appearance, demeanor, emotional state, attitude toward self, the interviewer, and the problem. This is vital not only for the overall assessment iself, but for caring for the client during the process. For example, if the client is a 14-year-old female who is reporting vaginal itching and discharge and seems nervous and uneasy about discussing the problem, the alert nurse will recognize the need for reassurance both before and during the pelvic examination. Careful observation guides the nurse in the professional interaction with the client and also helps direct the assessment.

Integration. The health history is not recorded just as received from the client. The nurse/interviewer is responsible for analyzing and sorting the information in order to write a concise, coherent narrative that is free of judgment and interpretation by the interviewer. Integration of the assessment is analogous to the phase in the writing process known as Planning (Chapter 3). The raw data received from the client must be analyzed and organized into a coherent pattern so that the written record will be both informative and intelligible.

Writing the History. Like all nurses' writing, the health history should be *precise, logical*, and *accurate* in presentation of the information. Each of these qualities, basic to all good writing in the clinical setting, is especially appropriate to the assessment.

BE PRECISE. In recording the "chief complaint" or reason for the visit, it is good practice to use the client's exact words. However, many clients respond with vague, general comments, and it is very important to write a comment that will be helpful in developing nursing care. But the nurse must resist the impulse to interpret for the client. Instead, try to elicit a more precise complaint. For example, if the client is asked:

"What brought you to the clinic today?"

and responds,

"I haven't felt well for a while"

the nurse cannot decide arbitrarily to write a more precise complaint but should explore the problem with the client until a more precise and helpful response can be recorded:

"I've felt weak and dizzy for the past four days, and I have no appetite."

This is not the time for diagnosis—whether the client's or the interviewer's. So if the client complains,

"My left elbow hurts when I do my housework. It's been about a week."

The nurse does *not* write:

"Bursitis of left elbow; one week duration"

but records the complaint as given by the client. On the other hand, if the client says,

"I think I have appendicitis,"

it is better to elicit the specific symptoms rather than accept the client's self-diagnosis and record:

"Nausea and loss of appetite for three days. Acute pain in lower abdomen for past 48 hours."

The chief complaint should be the symptoms as experienced by the client, not a diagnosis or assumption about the reason for the symptoms. The nurse's responsibility is to elicit a precise and clear complaint from the client and record it in equally precise and clear terms.

Throughout the health history precision is essential. The interviewer must establish precise information in relation to the current problem for subsequent diagnosis and plans. Often the client will not be aware of the type of information that is important, and it will be up to the nurse/interviewer to elicit the needed information. For example, a female client presents the complaint of "spotting," and the nurse knows that it is important to establish:

> How often?
> How much?

(In relation to quantity, it is best to estimate in terms of number of pads saturated in a given period of time or some other objective description that will help the client give a reliable estimate.)

If a client complains of "feeling dizzy," the precise interviewer will want to know:

> At all times?
> How frequently?
> When rising from bed?
> At any particular time of the day?

The reliability of the assessment is directly related to the nurse/interviewer's ability to elicit the most precise information.

BE LOGICAL. The History of Present Illness (HPI) is the narrative portion of the history which gives an elaboration of the chief complaint. It is important that this narrative be reported in some logical sequence. This can either be from the most recent episode sequentially back as far as the client can recall or from the origin of the problem (as far as the client can remember) up to the present. Either way is helpful and which one is used will depend on both the nature of the complaint and the client's manner of presentation, but it is important that if the client rambles the nurse be able to establish a logical sequence of events for the record.

BE ACCURATE. Part of the health history involves a past history in terms of childhood illnesses, immunizations, allergies, hospitalizations and serious illnesses, accidents and injuries, obstetric history, medications, etc. All dates should be ascertained as accurately as possible and recorded accurately, along with the name of the attending physician, location of hospitals, etc. It is particularly important for the nurse/interviewer to be alert to eliciting this information accurately as the client may not regard such items as significant if they are long past or are not directly associated with the current complaint.

Example of a Health History. **Figure 5-9** presents a typical health history. Note how the nurse has integrated the raw data into a

---

NAME ___N. M.___

ADDRESS _____

AGE ___71___ SEX ___M___ MARITAL STATUS ___M___

RACE _Caucasian_ RELIGION _____Catholic_____

OCCUPATION ___Civil engineer at consulting firm—full-time___

___since retirement 7 years ago.___

USUAL SOURCE OF MEDICAL CARE _General practitioner,_
ophthalmologist.

SOURCE AND RELIABILITY OF INFORMATION _Patient,_

who appears both articulate and reliable.

CHIEF COMPLAINT: "Chronic shortness of breath since childhood which has become gradually worse over the past year."

PRESENT ILLNESS: This 72-year-old man has considered

Figure 5-9. A completed health history. *(From Block ND; Health Assessment for Professional Nursing. New York, Appleton-Century-Crofts, 1981, pp 50-55. Reprinted with permission.)*

himself to be in good health. He does not feel dyspneic at the moment. As a child, he noticed he would become dyspneic following running sooner than his peers. During grade school and high school he had frequent absences due to bronchitis and asthma for which he was treated at home. During college he was well, but became short of breath with exertion, such as running or pushing a car. In (approximately) 1957, he had a lung capacity test done in Rochester, Minnesota, and was told he had 50 percent lung capacity. In 1969, the test was repeated and again he was told he had 50 percent lung capacity due to emphysema. There is no pain with inspiration, no coughing, no wheezing, no night sweats. Shortness of breath is only associated with exertion, such as lifting a moderately heavy box, walking fast, or playing golf on a hot day. He notices that less exertion causes shortness of breath than was required 1 year ago. When shortness of breath occurs, he ceases activity and it improves in 3 or 4 minutes. His work involves no real physical activity. He has an attack of "asthma" with wheezing 2 or 3 times a year. He uses "a squirt or 2" of Primatene Mist, which relieves symptoms. The asthma can be brought on by humid weather, cold weather, vapors from fried cooking, horses, cats, or excess dust. He does not consider his life stressful at present and also does not feel that anxiety ever precipitated an episode. He has never been formally tested for allergies. No interference with sleep.

For 20 years he smoked 2 to 2½ packs of cigarettes a day without inhaling. He stopped in 1954. He then smoked 2 cigars a day and stopped in 1969. He noticed no change in shortness of breath after he ceased smoking. He drinks 1 beer a day. Other than 2 uncomplicated surgical procedures (see section on Hospitalizations and Serious Illnesses), he has never been ill. His father had asthma and one of his sons has a history of asthma. He does not consider this disease life-threatening, just a "nuisance" which interferes with his golf game on occasion. Last chest x-ray 1973. Does not recall any "unusual comments from the doctor regarding the findings."

Figure 5-9. (Continued)

PAST HISTORY:

Childhood Illnesses: Chickenpox–under 10 years; "hard" measles–under 10 years; no history of German measles, mumps, strep throat, or scarlet fever. Bronchitis at least twice a year during grade school and high school.

Immunizations: Last remembers being immunized before college. Last tetanus shot 12/70.

Allergies: Vapors of fried cooking, animal hair, wheat (see HPI), caviar; none known to medications.

Hospitalizations and Serious Illnesses: 1943 hernia repair, no complications, Peoria, Illinois. 1945 bilateral vein ligation, no complications, Peoria, Illinois. In February, 1973, bronchoscopy at Wesley Hospital by Dr. Buckingham. At routine physical in January, 1973, "whistling" was heard on right frontal chest. It persisted following one month of cough medicine. "Laminar" chest x-rays were negative. Bronchoscopy negative.

Accidents: None.

Medications: Primatene Mist 2 to 3 times per year.

Habits: Not smoking presently, beer (1 × day), no other drug usage; 2 cups decaffeinated coffee per day; does not drink soda.

REVIEW OF SYSTEMS:

General: Height 6', Weight 180 lbs. Considers himself a "good weight." No recent gains or losses. Denies fatigue or weakness. Feels good, generally.

Skin: White flat elevations on chest and back present for 10 years. February, 1973 had some removed—none malignant. Have reappeared in greater number. Mild itching of skin on legs in the winter; treated with hand lotion. No rashes, lesions, tendency to bruising.

Figure 5–9. (Continued)

144

Hair: Gray, balding on frontal aspect, no dandruff.

Nails: No splitting, cracking, or biting.

Head: No headache, dizziness, or trauma. Occasional pain in anterior to right auricular area, enough to wake him at night. A sharp pain relieved after hot water bottle applied for ½ hour. Occurs approximately once a month for three-four years. Not associated with activity or weather. No treatment sought.

Eyes: Glasses for reading for 15 years. Sees ophthalmologist yearly for tonometry test. Was told his pressure is normally high. No diploplia, pain, history of infections, spots, photophobia, excessive lacrimation. No problems with night vision.

Ears: For past year, humming in both ears when he wakes mornings. Goes away when he gets up. No discharge, vertigo, earaches, or history of infections.

Nose and Sinuses: Mild epistaxis with colds when he blows his nose. No sinus pain, obstruction, discharge, post nasal drip, frequent colds, trauma, sneezing, or loss of smell.

Oral Cavity: No problems with teeth. No recent extractions, no soreness or bleeding of lips, gums, mouth, or tongue. Few sore throats, no disturbance of taste, no hoarseness. Sees dentist yearly.

Neck: No pain or limitation of motion, swelling, or history of goiter.

Nodes: No tenderness of cervical, axillary, or epitrochlear areas. Mild swelling in inguinal area first noticed by M.D. in 1969. No change—remains swollen. Was told it is like a varicose vein. No discomfort.

Breast: No pain, lumps, discharge.

Figure 5–9. (Continued)

Respiratory: See HPI.

Cardiovascular: No palpitation; dyspnea with exertion. Edema of both ankles 1971 to 1972, at end of day. He began wearing socks with loose tops and edema has not been present since 1973. No chest pain, orthopnea, paroxysmal nocturnal dyspnea, cyanosis, history of heart disease, murmur, rheumatic fever, palpitations, ↑ B.P., cramps, or varicose veins at present. (See Hospitalizations and Serious Illnesses section.)

Gastrointestinal: No history of abdominal pain or disease; no disturbance in appetite; no indigestion or food intolerances; no nausea, vomiting, belching, flatulence, or jaundice; no change in bowel habits or use of laxatives; has one formed brown stool daily. No diarrhea, constipation, use of laxatives, or hemorrhoids.

Genitourinary: No frequency, nocturia, polyuria, hesitancy, hematuria, or kidney stones; no history of UTI or V.D.

Back: No back stiffness, limitation of motion, or injury.

Extremities: No pain, swelling, redness, deformities of joints, crepitation, gout, limitation of movement, or history of fracture, injuries, or disease.

Neurologic: No speech disorder or change in sleep pattern; no tremors or weakness; no convulsions, loss of consciousness, strokes, mental illness, numbness, limps, paralysis, disorientation, mood swings, anxiety, depression, or phobias.

Hematopoietic: In 1957, was told he was anemic, asked to have test rerun as he did not believe diagnosis and then refused test. Took medication (iron) for 1 year. No tiredness. No bleeding tendencies or other blood diseases or transfusions.

Endocrine: No change in eating patterns. No unusual growth problems, thyroid problems, heat or cold intolerance,

Figure 5-9. (Continued)

146

polyuria, polydypsia, polyphagia. No change in glove or shoe size or hirsutism.

FAMILY HISTORY:

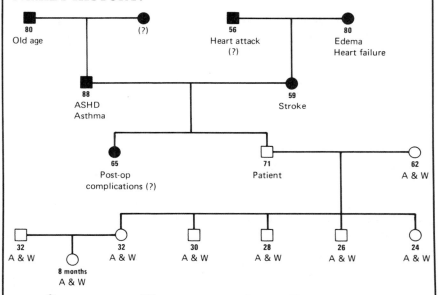

○ = female;   □   = male;   ● ,   ■   = deceased; no family history of cancer, diabetes, tuberculosis, epilepsy, mental illness, mental retardation, or kidney disease.

NUTRITIONAL HISTORY: Wife does all cooking and shopping. Tries to include "meat and vegetables" in diet daily. Dines out for dinner one time per month with wife and friends. Enjoys "all" foods, especially desserts. Two meals per day. Lunch—sandwich, fruit; dinner—meat, vegetables, potato, salad, dessert, and a glass of milk; 1 glass of beer in the evening.

Diet Yesterday: A.M.—1 cup of coffee; lunch—ham sandwich (2 pieces of white bread with mayonnaise and 3 slices of ham), 1 apple; snack—1 cup of coffee; dinner—2 slices pot

Figure 5-9. (Continued)

roast with gravy, 1 cup (or so) peas, 1 baked potato, 1 lettuce salad with dressing, 1 piece of apple pie with ice cream, 1 glass of milk; P.M. snack—1 glass of beer.

SOCIAL DATA:

Family Relationships and Friendships: Client feels "positive" about relationship with his family. He and his wife like one another both as people and as spouses: "There are 35 years of affection in our marriage." They talk over problems together and share decisions. His children are grown and he feels close to them. His first granddaughter was born 3 months ago and this gives him "a great thrill."

Ethnic Affiliation: Irish.

Occupational History: Worked for 40 years at L&R Railroad as a chief bridge engineer. Was required to retire in February, 1973 at 65 years of age. Started work full-time at consulting engineering firm the next week. Hopes to work until 75 years old and longer if his health remains good.

Educational History: Obtained B.S. and M.S. in Engineering at Fulton University.

Economic Status: Very happy that he found good employment following retirement. He is involved with different areas in his field which he has found challenging. Receiving retirement benefits. Feels economically secure at present. Helping children through graduate school as best he can.

Living Circumstances: Lives in two-bedroom home in a suburb of upstate New York. Has lived in this house for 23 years. He lives there with his wife. This home has gas heat, running water, etc. It is well insulated. There are no loose rugs, mats, etc. The house is easy to manage and he and his wife hope to live there until "our health gives out."

Pattern of Health Care: Sees his M.D. as needed and "every couple of years for a physical." Has eyes checked yearly

Figure 5-9. (Continued)

and also goes to the dentist annually. Doesn't have much faith in physicians. When he questions diagnosis or treatment, responses make him question their reliability. Has a complete record of all medical reports, bills, etc., since the early 1960s.

DEVELOPMENTAL HISTORY: Client and his wife feel financially secure for the future. They have arrangements with their children for their future residence, health needs, and other relevant concerns. He has strong religious beliefs which "give me courage when thinking of dying." Some of his children live nearby and they visit often. He is proud of his children and their accomplishments. He sees his life's goals as being fulfilled and still "learns new things about himself" every day.

SEXUAL HISTORY: Believes strongly in marital fidelity and feels he and his wife share very positive feelings about the sexual portion of their marriage.

PATIENT'S ACTIVITY TO REMAIN HEALTHY: Patient enjoys taking walks with his wife in the neighborhood when the weather permits. He relaxes by reading books in his field. Another favorite pastime is visiting with his family and granddaughter. He feels rest is essential to his "well-being" and retires by 10:00 P.M. every night.

Figure 5-9. (Continued)

precise, logical, and accurate narrative, using the client's own words wherever possible. Using the client's own words and phrases lessens the natural tendency to "editorialize" and interpret, which affects all professionals to some degree. In focusing on what the client reported, the nurse is reminded constantly that he or she is the analyzer or synthesizer of the data—but not the source. The written health history should represent the client's presentation of self as objectively as possible.

EXERCISES

I. Identify problems and write a nursing care plan for the hospital:

Assessment: Mark J. age 11 months has been admitted to the pediatric unit via the emergency department with a diagnosis of croup. His respirations are 35 per minute with an inspiratory wheeze. He is crying but is easily comforted by his mother. Temperature 102° F rectally, color pale, sweaty. Mother states she is "afraid he'll stop breathing."

II. Write the following nursing orders with appropriate abbreviations and symbols:

A. Soapsuds enema until clear.

B. Have patient turn, cough, and deep breathe every two hours.

C. Do passive range of motion exercises to lower extremities twice a day.

D. Irrigate foley catheter with 5000 cubic centimeters.

E. Keep right leg elevated 45 degrees.

III. You should be able to spell every word in this chapter. Assess your spelling ability in clinical practice. Plan a program of improvement as needed.

CHAPTER 6

Writing in the Academic Setting

Student nurses are confronted with a variety of writing assignments during the years of professional preparation for nursing practice. These assignments help introduce students to the nursing profession through papers on such topics as "Philosophy of Nursing" and "Issues in Nursing Practice," and help them develop competence as caregivers through client assessments and care plan analyses. Since the writing process remains a constant, regardless of the task, students who are familiar with the principles and skills covered in Chapters 1 to 4 will be more than adequately prepared for such assignments with regard to details of planning, style, and correctness. However, such "academic" writing often involves the presentation of information from secondary sources (survey of literature) or from the student's own research project. In both cases, although the basic writing process remains unchanged, more expertise is required, and the writer must become acquainted with the basic methodology for dealing with sources. That is the focus of this chapter.

Concepts of research are presented to students in most baccalaureate nursing programs, and most programs also regularly assign class papers and projects that require some type of "review of the literature." Often the literature review is the student's introduction to nursing research, and it is extremely important that the student understand how to review literature for specific purposes. The focus of the literature review will vary depending on whether it is being done as (1) a general background in formulating one's own research project; (2) a second review of the literature after one has stated a specific research problem; (3) a general exploration of a topic for a class essay. Since the class paper or project is usually the student's first encounter with the literature search, we will discuss the writing process as it functions in the preparation of such an expository essay.

THE CLASS PAPER

The major error in doing a review of the literature as part of an essay is in letting the literature *become* the essay. When consulting published sources, it is common for students to be overwhelmed by the polished prose of the printed article (not having seen the 27 revisions the author did to get to that point!) and hesitate to write a word of their own on the topic. The resulting "essay" is then a patchwork of various authors' perspectives on the topic, loosely strung together by the student. The true essay is the writer's *own* report; the literature is used to clarify, explain, or give direction to the topic under consideration. To make sure that the literature does not control the essay, the student must not go to the library too early in the process.

The first stage in the writing process, as in the nursing process, is assessment, and while assessment *includes* gathering data, that is only part of the assessment. It is essential that the writer begin with a preliminary assessment of the writing project as a whole before consulting sources. The place to begin is, once again, with our writer's triangle (see Fig. 1-1).

State Goal

Every writer, at all times, under all circumstances should come to terms with both subject and audience by stating a specific **goal**, as we discussed in Chapter 3. In the expository essay (one which primarily presents information), this goal may be simply the statement of purpose.

Example:

I am exploring the health problem of suicidal behavior in preadolescent children for my class project in Nursing 283.

Prewrite

It is also helpful for the writer to clarify his or her thoughts on the subject by writing something before the literature search is initiated as a type of personal assessment of attitudes or ideas. For example, the student who chose the topic of suicidal behavior in preadolescent children for a class project wrote this:

> Suicide is always a tragic event—especially when the victim is a young child. I had always thought that only adults committed suicide until I met Mildred and learned that her nine-year-old son died in an accident that was a suspected suicide. She told me that her pediatrician said that many young children have accidents that may really be suicide attempts. I wonder how they determine this and what can be done to prevent it? Is suicide in children very different from adult suicide?

This personal prewriting will probably never be part of the final essay, but it helps the writer to personally appropriate the subject and lessens the chance that he or she will be intimidated by the literature.

Plan

After assessing his or her views on the topic, the writer develops a tentative *plan*. Remember that you are not reporting on the literature itself but on the topic under consideration, so it is important to organize your presentation according to a logical presentation of the topic. This will also help direct your exploration of the literature. This is the plan the student developed to explore suicidal behavior among preadolescent children:

*Tentative Outline:**

Introduction
Definition(s)
Statistics
Causes
Management/treatment
Writer's conclusion

By articulating his or her own thoughts about the subject and developing a plan for the presentation of the topic, the student has assumed control of the project. Naturally, the literature search may require a modification of this initial framework, but the focus is on the presentation rather than the information. Data gathering is a component of the project—not an end in itself. The student's goal is to present the health problem in a logical and coherent manner. By developing a tentative plan *before* consulting the literature, the student/author is not dominated by the sources consulted.

Literature Search

The next stage is to consult the relevant literature. The first step is to consult reference works which "list" publications, such as indexes and bibliographies. Fortunately, there are many such sources for nursing and the related social science disciplines. The listing in Figures 6-1 and 6-2 show the important sources. From these indexes, the researcher can develop a list of possibly relevant sources (the working bibliography). At this stage of investigation, it is best to list more than fewer sources since titles of articles are often an unreliable indicator of content, and it is comparatively easy to retrieve journals for scrutiny. And, as one reads current articles, references are often made to "standard" works in the field, and the student can extend the working bibliography in this way as well.

CAUTION: In the excitement of discovery, it is common for the researcher to forget the details needed for source citation and regret it later. It is important to systematically copy the reference material that will be needed for the written citation. When you are at the

---

*Where an outline is given by the instructor, the assigned plan is used here.

Source	Information about Source	Period Covered by Source
NURSING		
Cumulative Index to Nursing and Allied Health Literature	Every 2 months with yearly cumulation. Glendale Adventist Medical Center Publications Service, Box 871, Glendale CA 91209. (Former title: Cumulative Index to Nursing Literature	1961 to date
Hospital Literature Index	Monthly with annual and 5-year cumulations. American Hospital Association, 840 N. Lake Shore Drive, Chicago IL 60611	1945 to date
International Nursing Index	Quarterly with annual cumulations. American Journal of Nursing Co., 10 Columbus Circle, New York NY 10019. (For the American Nurses' Association and National League for Nursing).	1966 to date
Nursing Research Index	A subject and author classification of studies published in *Nursing Research* each year. Appears in November–December issue	preceding year
Nursing Index	An annotated critical review of published studies and research-related materials in nursing	1900–1959
RELATED DISCIPLINES		
Abridged Index Medicus	Monthly with an annual cumulation. National Library of Medicine, 8600 Rockville Pike, Bethesda MD 20209	1970 to date
Bibliographic Index	A listing of bibliographies in 1,500 periodicals, by subject area, published annually, H.W. Wilson Co. 950	1943 to date

Figure 6–1. Indexes available in nursing, related disciplines, and popular literature *(From Fox DJ: Fundamentals of Research in Nursing, 4th ed. New York, Appleton-Century-Crofts, pp 100–01.)*

Source	Information about Source	Period Covered by Source
	University Avenue, Bronx, NY 10452	
Education Index	Most comprehensive guide to articles in educational journals. Gives a classified listing of titles	1929 to date
ERIC	An informational retrieval system supported by National Institute of Education. Indexes *and* abstracts published and unpublished research and so includes material not otherwise indexed	1965 to date
Index Medicus	Monthly with an annual cumulation. National Library of Medicine, 8600 Rockville Pike, Bethesda MD 20209	1960 to date
International Index	An index to American and foreign periodicals in the social sciences and humanities, with a heavy emphasis on political science, history and sociology, and little on education and psychology. New York: H.W. Wilson Co.	1961 to date
Science Citation Index	A unique approach to the indexing of over 2,600 journals from over 100 scientific fields. Based on the premise that a bibliography can be compiled by noting those current articles that cite (or refer to) an earlier published paper of known relevancy. Includes a Permuterm Subject Index (by key word). Institute for	1974 to date

Figure 6–1. (Continued)

Source	Information about Source	Period Covered by Source
	Scientific Information, 325 Chestnut Street, Philadelphia PA 19106. Six issues annually	
Social Science Index	An author and subject index to periodicals in the fields of anthropology, area studies, economics, environmental science, geography, law and criminology, medical sciences, political science, psychology, public administration, sociology and related subjects. Quarterly, New York: H.W. Wilson Co.	1974 to date
POPULAR LITERATURE Cumulative Book Index	A topical index of books published in the English language, published biannually at present. New York: H.W. Wilson Co.	1929 to date
New York Times Index	Twice monthly. Microfilming Corporation of America, P.O. Box 10, Sanford NC 27330	1913 to date
Readers' Guide to Periodical Literature	Twice monthly September to June, monthly July and August; annual cumulations, New York: H.W. Wilson Co.	1900 to date

Figure 6–1. (Continued)

stage of synthesizing your information and preparing the final draft of your paper, you don't want to have to go trudging back to the library to track down a page number that you forgot to note or the publisher's name that you have omitted. It is good practice to record the following information for every source you consult:

Source	Information about Source	Period Covered by Source
NURSING		
Nursing Research	Selected abstracts published each issue, subject classification, indexed annually in November–December issue	1960–1980
RELATED DISCIPLINES		
Biological Abstracts	References, abstracts and indexes to the world's life sciences research literature, BioSciences Information Service of Biological Abstracts, 2100 Arch Street, Philadelphia PA 19103. Semi-monthly	1926 to date
Chemical Abstracts	Chemical Abstracts Service (for the American Chemical Society) Box 3012, Columbus OH 43210. Weekly with annual cumulations	1907 to date
	Indexes and abstracts in English with new chemical information published in more than 500 languages. Covers over 14,000 journals, patents issued in 26 countries, books, conference proceedings, government reports, and dissertations	
Child Development Abstracts and Bibliography	Chicago, IL: Society for Research in Child Development, Inc. Abstracts of articles and bibliographies in area of child development, published three times a year.	1927 to date
Dissertation Abstracts (formerly Microfilm Abstracts)	Ann Arbor, MI: Edwards Brothers. Now published monthly. Starting with	1938 to date

Figure 6–2. Abstracting services in nursing and related disciplines. *(From Fox DJ: Fundamentals of Research in Nursing (4th ed). New York, Appleton-Century-Crofts, 1982, p. 102.)*

158

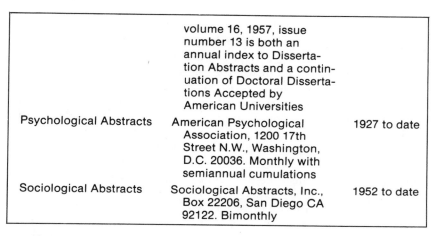

	volume 16, 1957, issue number 13 is both an annual index to Dissertation Abstracts and a continuation of Doctoral Dissertations Accepted by American Universities	
Psychological Abstracts	American Psychological Association, 1200 17th Street N.W., Washington, D.C. 20036. Monthly with semiannual cumulations	1927 to date
Sociological Abstracts	Sociological Abstracts, Inc., Box 22206, San Diego CA 92122. Bimonthly	1952 to date

Figure 6–2. (Continued)

Book

1. *Author's name*
2. *Complete title of book*
3. *Publisher*
4. *Place of publication (copyright)*
5. *Year of publication (copyright)*
6. *Total number of pages in the book*

Article

1. *Author*
2. *Title of article*
3. *Name of journal*
4. *Volume number and month and year of publication*
5. *Total pages covered by the article from the first to the last page on which it appears*

A good way to make sure that you copy the necessary material is to be systematic in your library work. If you are unfamiliar with the information you must note for each source, it's a good idea to prepare bibliography and note cards in advance if you have access to a ditto machine. Some university bookstores sell printed bibliography cards. Personally, we prefer using slips of paper cut to size rather than purchased index cards, as the former are cheaper and less bulky. It is also easier to ditto forms for your bibliography cards, to insure that you record all the required information. If you have no access to a ditto machine, prepare at least one "model" card for a book entry and one for a journal entry to refer to during your "search"—do not rely on memory or you may find yourself trekking back to the library in search of missing vital information. The bibliography cards need be no larger than 3 x 5 (Fig. 6–3).

You will want larger cards or slips for notes, perhaps 5 x 7. Note cards are to facilitate the integration of your source material into the final written paper. Do not record all the information from each source on one card, but record according to your outline. The writer who explored suicide among preadolescent children prepared note

Library Call No.

Author

Book Title   Edition

Publisher   City   Year

Pages of book (whole or part used)

Article Title

Name of Journal

        Volume   Month   Year

Figure 6–3. Sample bibliography card—writing down all the information you will need to cite your source helps minimize chances of omitting something during the process of research.

cards with the headings: Definition, Statistics, Causes, Management/treatment, and Miscellaneous (for information that may be needed for additional topics or for the writer's introduction or conclusion). Each note card is only used for one source but each source may have several different note cards (Fig. 6–4). The idea is that once the search is completed, the cards can be arranged by heading—e.g., all those dealing with "Definition"—for an easier synthesis of your sources. Whether you're in the library or at your typewriter, you're always writing your paper.

The review of the literature is not merely a library exercise. One nursing program evaluates the behaviors involved as follows:

> *The literature review:*
> **1.** *Evidences a thorough review of the literature which deals with the health concern being studied;*
> **2.** *Demonstrates an ability to select information appropriate to the topic;*
> **3.** *Communicates understanding of the literature in a logical style.*

It's clear that the first criterion is mainly a matter of time, energy, and efficiency, combined with a basic knowledge of library procedures. The second criterion involves the ability to discern relevant information while scanning many sources. Naturally, the preparing of a tentative outline is helpful in selecting appropriate sources. It is the third criterion, however, that is most often overlooked by those who consider the literature search confined to the library. The results must be *communicated* in some way, whether it is the paper that is written, the workshop that is presented, or the class that is taught. In the academic setting the results of the literature search most often are communicated in a "paper" or class project.

Writing the Paper

The paper which uses sources is theoretically no different from any other essay in the need for effective organization, cohesion, and correctness. However, in practice the integration of secondary sources is often a problem for writers. Part of this problem can be resolved through prior planning and effective note-taking. In the actual

```
┌─────────────────────────────────────────────┐
│  Causes                      Pfeffer          │
│                                                │
│     Study:  38% of 581 suicidal               │
│     children had been depressed for           │
│     at least 3 months prior to the            │
│     attempted suicide.                         │
│                                                │
│     Depression separated suicidal             │
│     from other chronically disturbed          │
│     children.                                  │
└─────────────────────────────────────────────┘

        ┌─────────────────────────────────────────────┐
        │    Causes                      Toolan         │
        │                                                │
        │       Childhood depression is an accepted     │
        │       psychiatric diagnosis.                   │
        │                                                │
        │       The Short Children's Depression          │
        │       Inventory (SCDI) is one particular       │
        │       psychological test used to evaluate      │
        │       the extent of depression in a child.     │
        └─────────────────────────────────────────────┘

┌─────────────────────────────────────────────┐
│  Causes                      Glaser           │
│                                                │
│    Depression is not a factor                 │
│    in suicidal behavior with                  │
│    children                                    │
│                                                │
│    (Challenged by Toolin)                      │
└─────────────────────────────────────────────┘
```

Figure 6-4. Sample note cards for "Causes" in student essay on preadolescent suicide.

writing of the paper, consistent style is the aim. This is sometimes difficult when you might be reporting the conclusions of ten different sources, all of which were written in their own individual styles. The key to a consistent style is to use your own words as much as possible—paraphrase, paraphrase, paraphrase. For precise definitions or statistics you may need to quote a phrase or sentence directly, but avoid direct quotation otherwise, as it tends to break the natural flow of language. Note, for example, how the writer of the paper on suicide among preadolescent children skillfully integrates her sources in the first four paragraphs of her essay (note too how these paragraphs correlate with sections 1–3 of her tentative outline:

> The issue of suicide is filled with emotional connotations, and childhood suicide in particular is especially hard to deal with. For that reason and others, suicide in children is a subject which, until lately, has been neglected. There has been a tendency among social scientists and psychiatrists to see suicidal acts as accidents resulting from the child's impulsive nature. It is easier to rationalize than to confront the fact that children can contemplate taking their own lives.
>
> For the purpose of this discussion, a few definitions and statistics are in order. Suicidal behavior includes thoughts and/or actions that if fully carried out, may lead to serious self-injury or death. The spectrum of suicidal behavior runs from suicidal ideation, suicidal threats, suicidal attempts, to completed suicide (Pfeffer, Feb., 1981).
>
> Rosalie Tyrrell, in an article on self-poisoning in children (June, 1980), further defines suicidal behavior. She divides suicide attempts into three categories. "Just talk" is the least threatening way for a child to announce his intent. If this occurs frequently, it should be evaluated. The "gesture" is a more pronounced signal for the purpose of influencing another and, through him, to control his environment. More serious attempts will follow if action is not taken here. "Threats" are more serious, but hard to distinguish from "just talk." They must be evaluated in light of the child's history. The "attempt" is often the last desperate warning given by the child, and is occasionally fatal.

Statistics show that suicide in young children is on the rise. In 1955, there were 0.4/100,000 deaths in children 10–14 years old. In 1975, that number had risen to 1.2/100,000 deaths in the same age group. In the late 1960s, it was estimated that 7–10 percent of children seen in psychiatric clinics had suicidal symptoms, whereas in 1980, one New York clinic reported that of 39 children randomly chosen, 33 percent had contemplated, threatened, or tried suicide (Pfeffer, Feb., 1981).

Note how clear and direct the style of this essay is. The expository essay aims to *present* the topic, as opposed to the narrative form which is intended to tell a story—e.g., "Why I chose nursing as a career" or "How we solved the problem of the difficult patient in Room 506." The narrative is usually based in personal experience and is more subjective in content. For example, the student's prewriting for this topic of preadolescent suicide, though helpful in planning her project, could not be incorporated in the final essay as it was essentially narrative, the wrong "style."

Although the expository essay should be clear and direct, it should not be dull and boring. Since the writer aims to inform the reader, he or she also wants the reader to finish the essay. However, the expository essay, unlike the narrative, does not rely on suspense or personal revelation to gain reader interest. Since the purpose is to inform, nothing should be too subtle or "left to the reader's imagination." Note how in the paragraphs quoted from this student essay the topic sentence *begins* the second, third, and fourth and appears very near the beginning of the first paragraph as well. The effectiveness of the expository essay is largely a result of good organization. The student who would like to review that aspect of the writing process should see Chapter 3.

A word must be said about diction as well. Although the nurse is most often writing for other health care professionals, the language of an expository essay should never be excessively technical or full of jargon. The essay's purpose is communication. Students who want to sound educated and professional are especially prone to this fault that might be termed "overwriting." This is common in nursing which has a specialized vocabulary. That vocabulary must be used but not abused.

Some reminders about style (style is covered more basically in Chapter 4):

- **Never multiply words**— if you can say it in fewer words, use fewer words.
- **Never choose a big word when a small one will be just as precise.** Precision is the key here. Often in nurses' writing the "big" word *is* needed. "Diaphoretic" is a perfectly reasonable adjective that cannot be precisely communicated in one small word.
- **Never sacrifice clarity for cleverness.** The purpose is to inform, not entertain.
- **Avoid lengthy sentences.** Meaning tends to get muddled when sentences get too complex.

In preparing class assignments that call for a review of the literature, students would do well to remember the **5 Ps:**

Prepare	State your goal clearly and precisely
Prewrite	Explore and/or clarify your thoughts about the topic briefly in writing
Plan	Develop a tentative outline for the presentation of the topic and prepare appropriate note cards for your library work
Ponder	Review the literature thoroughly, selecting appropriately for your topic
Present	Communicate in a clear, logical essay

This simple scheme provides a basic implementation of the writing process for papers or projects that call for a search of the literature.

THE RESEARCH PROJECT

Today, research is a basic component in nursing education. The professional nurse must be able to predict within reasonable limits what will be the outcomes of specific nursing interventions. This cannot be done without examining practice. Whether as a consumer or producer, every professional nurse is involved with the reality of research and must be educated in research methods and procedures. This book does not attempt to teach the fundamentals of nursing research. That topic requires book-length consideration, and at the end of this chapter we have listed several books which provide excellent instruction for the baccalaureate student or any novice researcher. In this chapter, we will emphasize the ways in which the writing process interfaces with the research process concentrating on the writing skills needed by the nurse/researcher.

In developing the research project, it may initially seem that the emphasis is on methodology rather than writing. For example, as we look at a typical presentation of the research process (Fig. 6–5), it appears that the actual writing (Step 18) is merely one step among the 20. However, since research is a problem-solving process, it has explicit analogy to the writing process, and many of the steps in the development of the research plan are already familiar to the writer who has had experience in formulating and limiting a topic for class papers.

Every research project is basically a three-stage process:

1. Designing the plan
2. Collecting the data
3. Writing the report

and writing skills are especially important to the first and final stages.

Designing the Plan

While many texts speak of the "tension" between the nurse/practitioner and the nurse/researcher, those roles are essentially complementary insofar as the writing process is concerned. The nurse in the clinical care setting must be accurate, precise, and complete in recording client information, and the nurse engaged in research must be similarly accurate, precise, and complete in designing, implementing, and reporting on a research project. The process of developing the research plan is one of progressively narrowing to focus on the *specfic* and *precise* description of what will be done.

The initial idea and problem area are analogous to the topic of

AN OVERVIEW OF THE RESEARCH PROCESS

Part One: Designing the Research Plan

Stage 1. Developing the ethical framework
Stage 2. The initiating idea and the problem area
Stage 3. Defining the purpose of the research
Stage 4. The initial review of the literature: estimating success potential
Stage 5. Delineating the population(s) to be studied
Stage 6. Stating the specific research problem and defining terms
Stage 7. The second review of the literature and stating hypothesis
Stage 8. Selecting the research approach
Stage 9. Selecting the data-gathering method and technique and developing the data-gathering instrument(s)
Stage 10. Developing the data-analysis plan including statistics
Stage 11. Selecti. g the sample to be invited to participate
Stage 12. Pilot studies of techniques of data collection, data-gathering instruments, and the methods of data analysis
Stage 13. Identifying the assumptions and limitations of the research
Stage 14. Designing the data-gathering plan
Stage 15. Inviting the selected sample to participate

Part Two: Implementing the Research Plan

Stage 16. Implementing the data-gathering plan
Stage 17. Implementing the data-analysis plan

Part Three: Reporting and Applying the Results

Stage 18. Preparing the research reports
Stage 19. Application of results
Stage 20. Agitation for action

Figure 6–5. Stages of the research process in nursing research. *(From Fox, DJ: Fundamentals of Research in Nursing, 4th ed. New York, Appleton-Century-Crofts, 1982, pp. 26–27.)*

an essay. The researcher is usually attracted to a specific interest area and investigates the literature within that area to see if there is something that needs to be examined further. For example, Joan DiPasquale is a nurse who works with mentally retarded adults in a transitional living situation. That became her primary area of interest when designing a research project for her M.S.N. Mary Friel is a student nurse who has had experience working with physically disabled individuals as a volunteer. She is interested in issues relating to the disabled, and may develop a senior research project in that area. To go from 'interest" to specific research problem is like the writer moving from goal to controlling idea (see Chapter 3). This is the reason for the first literature review. While the researcher often has personal experience in the area of investigation and some preliminary knowledge of the basic issues in that area, he or she explores the literature to determine what has been done and what needs to be investigated. With the aid of this exploration of the kinds of studies that have been done in the area of interest and their results, the researcher then formulates a statement of his or her specific research problem.

Specificity, always important in writing, is especially vital here. The researcher must define every key word, so that there is a common understanding of precisely what is meant. For example, Joan DiPasquale's research project was titled "A Comparison of the Effects of Two Teaching Methods on the Community Living Skills of Educable Mentally Retarded Adults," and she offered specific definitions of the following terms:

1. Individual teaching method
2. Group teaching method
3. Community living skills
4. Educable
5. Mentally retarded

Once the key terms have been defined, the researcher must be sure to use them consistently throughout the project and subsequent report. This is an important aspect of writing in relation to research. The student writer is generally advised to vary diction and use synonyms for recurring words. However, this is not a preference in scientifically based writing. Just as the clinician does not casually substitute "belly" for "abdomen" for variety, the researcher is similarly consistent in using precise terminology throughout the project.

After the researcher has articulated his or her specific research problem, there is usually a second review of the literature from this more focused perspective. The researcher is now ready to take notes for the eventual "review of the literature" which will be part of the final research report. And as the researcher explores the work of others in this area, formulating the specific approach to this developing project may be facilitated. The stages of assessment and planning, integral to both the nursing and writing processes, are continually employed during this phase of project design, until they culminate in the researcher's readiness to implement the project.

Implementing the Plan

Often research is thought of as *primarily* the activity involved in implementing the plan, but, in fact, the major task of the researcher is the project design as Figure 6–5 indicates. There are far fewer decisions to be made during the implementation phase of the project since, with the exception of unexpected developments or emergency situations, the implementation is precisely and specifically dictated by the design.

Reporting the Results

Although at this stage of the research project the researcher should feel that he or she is "home free," writing the report is traditionally more of a task than it should be. For some reason (perhaps the natural fear of exposing one's "child" to an evaluating audience), writing up the results of original research engenders writer's block for many people. The researcher should be prepared for this phenomenon and overcome it with the realization that although writing a research report is a specialized writing task, the basic elements of the writing process are still operative. Essentially the report is designed to inform a relevant audience of the decisions, details, and conclusions of the research project. The same basic writer's triangle is operative (Fig. 6–6).

Considerations of Form. Probably most report writing fear stems from the fact that form is such a formidable foe. From high school research paper days when students struggled with the differences between footnote form and bibliography form and tried

RESEARCHER/WRITER

RESEARCH
DATA

RELEVANT
AUDIENCE

Figure 6-6. The researcher employs the same basic writer's triangle.

to decide how to cite a book with three authors and two different places of publication, form has loomed as more of a bugbear than it should. Quite simply, where citation is concerned we follow the prescribed handbook. Several of the commonly used handbooks are given in the resource list appended to this chapter. The particular handbook used is customarily chosen by the nursing program or the faculty advisor, but, in any case, citation is simply a matter of intelligently consulting and following the handbook.

The form of the report itself is also determined by either the department or the advisor. Typically, a research project report will be divided into eight sections:

1. Introduction and problem statement
2. Review of the literature
3. Hypothesis
4. Design of the study and procedure for data gathering including a description of the data-gathering instruments and the sample used
5. Results of the study

6. Discussion of the results
7. Conclusions
8. Suggestions for further research

As is apparent from this listing, the first four items are part of the project design. It is a good idea to write these steps in draft form before the implementation of the project. Having a portion of the written report "in progress," helps banish writer's block. The writing up of the report should not become an added problem in the research project. Rather, the writing of the report should be considered a cohesive whole, begun with the initial idea and completed with the suggestions for further research.

Considerations of Style. The report is not intended as a "product" to display the researcher's expertise but as a means of communication among professionals. Therefore the writing is clear and direct, avoiding obfuscating jargon. Like all nurses' professional writing, the report should be accurate, consistent, and thorough. The researcher who has spent a great deal of time designing and implementing a project will *want* to communicate the results, and the writing style should be direct and energetic to suggest that the information being conveyed is interesting and valuable.

Since the research report is expository prose, the first four chapters of this book provide sufficient background for writing the report. The student who is familiar with the nature of the writing process and the basic considerations of correctness, planning, and style which have been discussed in Chapters 1 to 4 is amply prepared. There are just a few caveats:

- **Write in a clear, direct style.** From the first words of the introduction, the researcher should concentrate on communicating results. There is no need to pique the reader's interest with an opening anecdote. Assume the reader is genuinely interested in the substance of your report, and get right to the point. The introduction would do well to begin with "This study was intended to . . ." or some similar formulation.
- **Be precise and consistent.** Remember to define clearly and use all key terms consistently throughout the report. Avoid all excessively technical diction.

- **Do not use the first person.** Research writing is impersonal. Refer to yourself as the "investigator" or the "researcher," *not* the "writer" since that is not your primary role in the project. To keep the writing impersonal, it is helpful to use the passive voice (usually otherwise avoided in written communication). Instead of "I thought that. . ." say, "It was thought that ..." Instead of "I conducted an investigation. . ." say, "An investigation was conducted. . . ."
- **Be careful of verb tenses.** Since the report is written after all the planning, researching, and implementation has been completed, all is reported in the past tense. The future tense is appropriately used for the hypothesis and suggestions for further research. The present tense is only used for internal references to the data, e.g., "The results listed in Table 4 indicate that. . . ."

A Final Note. Do not expect to sit down at the typewriter and instantly compose a lively and readable research report. The level of precision and consistency required in a properly done report comes only after much editing and revision. As a student you will always be writing against a deadline. Allow sufficient time for such revision. You do not want all the time and energy spent in designing and implementing a research project to result in a poorly prepared report. The research report should adequately reflect the skill and care you have put into the entire project.

SELECTED RESOURCES

The following items will be especially helpful to the baccalaureate student nurse involved in the prepartion of academic papers:

The Literature Search:
Binger JL, Jensen LM: Lippincott's Guide to Nursing Literature. Philadelphia, JB Lippincott Co., 1980.
Strauch KP, Brundage DJ: Guide to Library Resources for Nursing. New York, Appleton-Century-Crofts, 1980.

Documentation:

American Psychological Association, Council of Editors. Publication Manual of the American Psychological Association (2nd ed). Washington, D.C., American Psychological Association, 1974.

University of Chicago: A Manual of Style (12th ed). Chicago, University of Chicago, University of Chicago Press, 1960.

Research Methodology:

Brink PJ, Wood MJ: Basic Steps in Planning Nursing Research: From Question to Proposal. North Scituate, MA, Duxbury Press, 1978.

Fox DJ: Fundamentals of Research in Nursing (4th ed). New York, Appleton-Century-Crofts, 1982.

Pavlovich N: Nursing Research: A Learning Guide. St. Louis, Mosby, 1978.

Polit DF, Hungler BP: Nursing Research: Principles and Methods. Philadelphia, JB Lippincott Co., 1978.

CHAPTER 7

Writing in the Professional Setting

The nursing student who has mastered the components of the writing process is well prepared for the various writing experiences he or she will encounter as a professional nurse. As with the nursing process, successful application of the principles involved in the writing process develops with experience. Just because you never cared for a patient with a depressed skull fracture during your clinical experience in nursing school, does not mean that you cannot adequately care for such a patient. You might need to review some basic procedures, but your understanding of the nursing process prepares you to deal with individual health concerns as you encounter them.

The same is true of the writing process. The student nurse who has learned to write correctly and clearly with precision and appropriate style is adequately prepared for all professional writing experiences. Successful writing for such an individual is a matter of keeping the basics in mind and becoming aware of the specific requirements of each writing task. In this chapter we will discuss writing experiences that confront the newly graduated nurse—writing business letters (especially letters of application), preparing a résumé, and writing memos. We will also consider another increasingly important element in the nursing profession—the preparation of articles and books.

CORRESPONDENCE

A most important consideration in preparing professional correspondence is *appearance*. The business letter or memo is a reflection
of you as a professional. Just as you would not appear on the
clinical care unit with a soiled uniform and uncombed hair, you
should never present yourself as "unkempt" in your professional
correspondence. This means that you use good quality bond paper
and type neatly. There should not be any trace of the unevenness of
a worn-out ribbon, no strikeovers or noticeable corrections. Use
standard 8-1/2 x 11 paper and type only on one side of the paper.
Whether you are writing to a client, another health care professional, an agency, or a funding s urce, when you are writing in your
role as a professional nurse, the tone of your letter should reflect
that fact. The business letter is not overly friendly nor is it excessively formal. There has been an increasing tendency toward
informality over the past years (as our society as a whole has
become more informal), and this means that the more stilted phrasing once characteristic of business correspondence has been
eliminated.

NOT	**BUT**
"It is my humble opinion that. . . ."	"I think that. . . ."
"The aforementioned client. . . ."	"The client. . . ."
	or
	"Mr. Clancy. . . ."
"The very excellent article which I was so privileged to read in your journal. . . ."	"The excellent article on pain management in your January issue. . . ."

Like *all* nurses' writing, professional correspondence should be
accurate, clear, and precisely formulated.

Every professional, whether it be nurse, physician, lawyer,
architect, or engineer, should be familiar with the standard forms of
the business letter. Even if correspondence is prepared by a secre-
tary, you must be able to certify as correct any letter that goes out
with your signature. Figure 7-1 illustrates the form of the standard
business letter. Note the format. Any correspondence you initiate as
a professional nurse should be as correct as your charting.

Format

The business letter has six basic parts (Fig. 7–1):

1. Heading
2. Inside address
3. Salutation
4. Body
5. Closing
6. Any added notations

The heading includes the full address of the writer and the date of the letter. Note that the heading has no end punctuation. When writing for your agency, you may be using letterhead stationery with a printed name and address. In this case, only the date is typed (about three spaces below the letterhead and beginning at the center of the page). The month is always written in full:

December 9, 1982; *not* Dec. 9, 1982; *never* 12/9/82.

The inside address gives the name and address of the person to whom the letter is being written. The space between the heading and the inside address is variable (usually four to six lines) and is determined by the space needed to center the letter neatly on the paper.

The salutation greets the person to whom the letter is addressed. The appropriate greeting is important, so the following guidelines should be kept in mind:

1. When the surname of the addressee is known, it is used with the appropriate title:

Dear Mrs. Calloway:
Dear Captain Gonzalez:
Dear Dr. Kerr:
Dear Professor Blattner:

Note: *Use Miss or Mrs. if the woman you are addressing has indicated a preference; in all other cases use Ms. which is always appropriate.*

262 Overdale Street
Morgantown, WV 26505
November 5, 1982
┐
├── HEADING
┘

INSIDE   ┌ Saundra Powley, R.N., Coordinator
ADDRESS ─┤ Cardio-Pulmonary Care Program
         │ County Hospital
         └ Morgantown, WV 26505

SALUTATION ── Dear Ms. Powley:

       ┌ I read with great interest the notice of your new program which appeared in
       │ last Sunday's *Dominion Post.* My father has been ill with emphysema for
       │ several years, and has many of the breathing problems that were mentioned in
       │ that article. His physician, Dr. Michael Lambert, has already suggested that my
       │ father enroll in your program, but he refuses to consider it.
BODY ──┤
       │   Do you have any type of pamphlet or other literature about your program
       │ that would be helpful in convincing my father that he could benefit from this
       │ therapy? Perhaps you would be willing to let me bring him in for an informal visit.
       └ Please let me know if there is any help you can offer in this situation.

I can be reached by phone (293-3107) weekdays from 9–4 and at my home (292-4925) evenings and weekends. I have learned a great deal about respiratory illness during the years since my father developed emphysema, and I know that your program is most valuable. Perhaps together we can convince my father.

Very truly yours,

Lillian Carter

 CLOSING

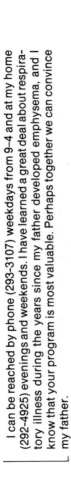 (no notations)

Figure 7-1. A letter prepared by an individual in indented style.

179

2. In letters to organizations or to persons whose name and sex are unknown, the following types of salutations are appropriate:

Dear Nurse Recruiter:
Dear Director of Nurses:
Dear Editor:
Dear Admissions Committee:
Dear Sir or Madam: *(When sex is known but not name,*
                      either Dear Sir or Dear Madam is
                      always appropriate.)

For very particular situations, most dictionaries list "Forms of Address" including the proper greeting for everyone from an abbot to a widow. It's a valuable resource.

The body contains the message of the letter. Typewritten letters (and all professional correspondence should be typewritten) are single-spaced with double spacing between paragraphs. Paragraphs should be written in a clear, direct style. There is no place for ambiguity or subtlety in business correspondence.

The closing ends the letter and includes the following:

1. *The complimentary close—the conventional ending which is typed three lines below the last paragraph in the body of the letter. This is either more or less formal depending on the nature of the letter.*

Formal
Yours truly,
Very truly yours,

Less Formal
Sincerely,
Cordially,

Note: *The spelling of "truly," is one of the most commonly misspelled parts of the letter!)*

2. *The typed name as it will be written is spacèd four* *lines below the closing. Your title is added only if you are writing in an official capacity.*

Phyllis Weiss
Chairperson, Recruitment Committee

David Ingles
Medical Coordinator

Stella Morris
Director of Educational Services

3. *The signature is placed between the complimentary close and the typed name.*

Added notations are typed flush with the left margin and are used to indicate whether or not something is enclosed or attached to the letter (enc., att.), to whom copies of the letter have been sent (cc. Jean Morganstern), the initials of the author and typist of the letter (CKJ:tal).

Form
There are three basic styles for business letters and they correspond to level of formality:

Full block	Most formal	Used mainly by business
Modified block	Less formal	Used mainly by business or officials
Indented	Least formal	Used mainly by individuals

In full block all parts of the letter are flush with the left margin. The modified block style, more common, moves the heading and the complimentary close to the right while all else is flush with the left margin. Paragraphs are not indented. Indented style is like the modified block but with paragraphs indented (Fig. 7-2). When you are writing as an individual, e.g., in a letter of application, the indented style is most appropriate. When you are writing for your agency, you should use the agency's preferred form.

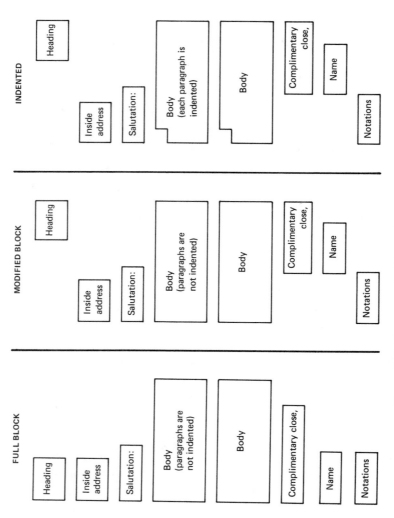

Figure 7-2. Three standard forms for the business letter.

The Letter of Application

Probably the most "important" correspondence the newly graduated nurse will initiate is the letter of application. While the emotional involvement in this task may be intense, this is actually an easy form of business correspondence because the elements of the basic writer's triangle are so clearly defined (Fig. 7–3).

There are two main types of letters of application: solicited and unsolicited. A solicited letter of application is one written in response to a specific position that has been advertised in some way. You may have seen an ad for the job in a newspaper or journal, or you may have learned about it from supervisors or other nurses. There is a position available and applications are expected. The unsolicited letter is initiated by the sender without any action on the part of the agency. Often the nurse has a reason for wanting to work with a particular agency or in a particular area and will send a letter of application to inquire as to whether or not there is a suitable position available. Both types of application letters are acceptable and are regularly received by health care agencies.

The letter of application is designed to have the employer look

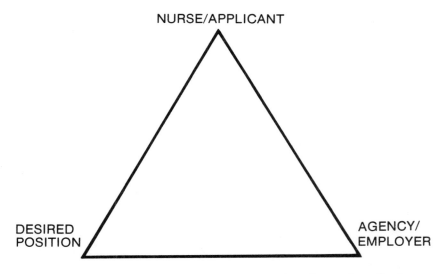

Figure 7–3. The dynamics of the writing process for a letter of application.

carefully at your résumé and grant you an interview. The letter is particularly important as it is the first presentation of yourself. Unlike the résumé which is a general professional biography, the letter of application allows you to respond specifically to a particular position (solicited letter) and/or give more details of your professional interests and goals. It is more personal than the résumé. Remember that your letter of application is designed to *complement* rather then *duplicate* your résumé. You do not just list your accomplishments in a narrative form. Instead, the letter of application has three main parts:

1. *Identify the position you are applying for and state how you heard about the opening.* If the letter is unsolicited, explain why you are applying to this particular agency—i.e., location, reputation, opportunities for specialization or further education, etc.
2. *Extend your résumé by offering details about your experience pertinent to this particular position.* The nurse who has just received a B.S.N. should not simply list courses taken—unless they were extremely specialized and appropriate to the position. The new graduate should refer to placement experience or volunteer work or identify clinical areas of interest. A recently graduated student is not expected to have extensive experience.
3. *Give references or state where they may be obtained, and offer availability for an interview.* It is best to be tactful about the latter. No matter how anxious you are for any particular position, avoid saying things like "I hope you will want to interview me at your convenience" or "I can come for an interview anytime." Be accommodating but professional, especially if the position is located in another geographic area that means traveling expenses for you. You might say, for example, "I will be in Washington for the ANA Convention next month and will be available for an interview at that time" or "I will be available for an interview any time during the week of April 8th." Even for local interviews you should indicate specific times of availability. For example, "I am available for interviews on Mondays and Fridays during the next

month." You need not add, "because I don't have classes those days" or "those are my days off." It is not necessary to offer such information.

Remember, too, that you should obtain prior permission from anyone you use as a reference.

As in all other nurses' professional writing, this letter should be accurate and precise. You are asking for an interview, and while you should be direct, you must avoid the pitfalls of being either excessively bold (see Chapter 4) or exceedingly obsequious. Avoid saying, "Your search is over!" or "I'm perfect for this job." But also avoid such "humble" sentences as "I hope you will find my credentials adequate for the excellent opportunity you advertise," or "Although I don't really deserve to be a team leader, I will do the best I can if you hire me."

Your letter of application should not be longer than one typewritten page. If your letter "has to" be longer, you're saying too many unnecessary things or your writing is too wordy. In either case, serious revision is called for. Figures 7-4 and 7-5 illustrate letters of application written by nurses, one beginning his professional career, the other with several years' experience. One important caveat with regard to letters of application: It is inappropriate and unprofessional to apply for positions for which you clearly do not have the education or experience required, no matter how confident you may be of your ability.

Remember that a letter of application should be tailored to a particular audience and so should *never* be a standard form letter that you have duplicated. No matter how many positions you're applying for, each letter of application should be individually prepared for the particular position or agency to which it is directed. Your résumé, on the other hand, is a standard professional biography and is best duplicated professionally. Most of the concerns that do printing or copying will set up your résumé from the information you furnish for a slight extra charge. This is a wise investment because the professional layout with varied typefaces is vastly superior to the résumé that can be produced at home with a standard typewriter. But while you need not master the *typing* of your résumé, you must master the essential components of a professional résumé.

72 Harding Avenue
New York, NY 11372
July 2, 1983

Josephine Stillwell
Personnel Director
Twin Oaks Hospital
Old River, New York 11726

Dear Ms. Stillwell:

I am writing in response to your advertised position in the July issue of *Nursing 83*. As you can see from my enclosed résumé, psychiatric nursing is my primary area of interest, and I would like to gain experience in a small psychiatric hospital like Twin Oaks. I will take my state boards on July 10 and 11 and could start immediately afterwards.

I just received my B.S.N. from New York University, and during my senior year I chose psychiatric nursing as my clinical specialty. In addition to participating in a special seminar in psychiatric nursing, I did a placement in the psychiatric unit at Bellevue Hospital and in University Hospital's Alcoholic Rehabilitation Unit. This experience seems appropriate for the position you describe.

My enclosed résumé lists references. I am available for an interview weekdays during the next month. I look forward to hearing from you.

Yours truly,

Patrick Ryan

Enc. Résumé

Figure 7-4. A letter of application from a newly graduated nurse. (See Fig. 7-6 for Patrick Ryan's résumé.)

201 Beech Street
Morgantown, West Virginia
November 14, 1982

David Forrest, Administrator
County Hospital
Morgantown, West Virginia 26505

Dear Mr. Forrest:

I have been informed by Dr. Stephen Westfall that County Hospital is planning to establish a geriatric center and is currently searching for a suitable director to help plan the center and eventually administer it. I am writing to apply for that position. I have been involved in geriatric nursing in this area for the past five years and hold both a B.S.N. and a Certificate in Gerontology from West Virginia University. I am currently enrolled in the M.S. program in health education and administration and expect to receive that degree in 1984.

As my enclosed résumé indicates, I have broad experience in geriatric nursing in both a large city hospital and in private nursing homes. For the past three years, I have had administrative responsibilities as supervisor at Mountain State Nursing Home. I have also become acquainted with the needs of older citizens through my work with the county's Senior Citizens' Council and would welcome the opportunity to contribute to the establishment of a new geriatric center at County Hospital which would serve this population.

My complete dossier is available from the Professional Credentials and Personnel Service offered through the ANA. I am available for an interview anytime on Mondays; other times can be arranged if necessary. I look forward to hearing from you.

Sincerely yours,

Margaret Steiner

MS/bk
Enc. Résumé

Figure 7–5. A letter of application from a nurse with several years' experience. (See Fig. 7–7 for Margaret Steiner's résumé.)

The Résumé

One of the major changes in recent years is that the type of information standard on a résumé a generation ago is now no longer required—and is unprofessional when offered. The only personal information you offer is your name, mailing address, and a phone number where you can be reached. *Never* add such items as birth date, sex, marital status, height and weight, and do not include a photograph. You should be considered for employment on your professional qualifications, and the following areas of *professional* concern are addressed:

Registration. Registered nurses should always include the name of the state in which their boards were taken and their registration number. Nurses who are licensed in more than one state should include multiple registrations. The student who is applying for a first job and may not yet have taken state boards should indicate when they will be taken.

Education. This is listed in reverse chronological order, with the last degree achieved listed first. The baccalaureate student who expects to graduate in June and is applying for positions in April may write:

B.S.N.   West Virginia University   June 1982

This should not be done more than three months before graduation. You do not list the courses you've taken for the degree, but any special training beyond the standard nursing program should definitely be included. Double majors or minors should also be mentioned. If a nurse has graduated from a diploma school or an AD program and gone on for a B.S.N., that former education should also be listed. Since this is a professional biography, it is not necessary to include high school but only that education which was specific preparation for nursing.

Honors. Professional recognition is an important sign of competence and superior qualifications—things a potential employer will value. Any honors, scholarships, or awards should be included as part of your professional status.

Experience. This is also reported in reverse chronological order (present or latest position first) and is listed by name of agency, dates employed, title held, and (if appropriate) a brief description of the duties involved. Student should include any internships, placement experience, and any volunteer experience that is health related. This need not be extensive, as the résumé of a newly graduated nurse will understandably not indicate much experience.

Clinical Areas of Interest. This will complement and personalize the nurse's experience. Included here are those areas (it is best to limit to a maximum of three) in which the nurse has either (1) special interest; (2) additional training; or (3) extensive involvement. The student should list those areas in which he or she would *choose* to develop experience and/or receive further education.

Professional Organizations. Such memberships indicate active, professional nurses. Individuals should also indicate if they serve on committees or held office in such organizations. Students should indicate if they were members of student nurse organizations.

Civic Organizations. Nurses, like other professionals, are members of the broader local community and should indicate that involvement to prospective employers. Even such non-nursing activities as member of the public library board or representative to the city council are indications of character and interests and help reflect the whole person.

Conferences and Workshops. The titles, dates, and locations of conferences and workshops attended are listed with the most recent first. Titles are put in quotation marks. The presenter or leader is usually not mentioned unless the person is of national importance and conducted a workshop in which you received specific instruction. If *you* conducted a workshop or delivered a paper at a conference, these are listed separately as "Workshops Conducted" and "Papers Delivered."

Research. Any research done as either a thesis or dissertation should be listed here as well as projects done under a grant of any kind or as consultation.

Publications. Journal articles, chapters in books, monographs, and books are listed with proper bibliographic form.

References. At least four references should be given. These are people who will testify to your professional competence and personal sense of responsibility. Obviously, supervisors and clinical instructors are good choices for students. More experienced nurses should choose head nurses, directors of nursing, and others who have supervised their work. It is also correct and advisable to include personal references, especially clergy or teachers. Naturally, you must ask these people if they would be willing to supply references before you list their names. Some nurses have their credentials on file with the American Nurses Association Professional Credentials and Personnel Services which supplies references to employers at the member's request. Those nurses should simply cite this on their résumé without listing the references.

This detailed inventory should not intimidate the student or newly graduated nurse. Every item mentioned will not be included unless the individual has relevant experience. For example, if the nurse has not published, he or she does *not* list:

Publications: None

but simply omits that section. The vital areas of concern to a prospective employer are education, experience, and references. All other details are included as appropriate. Most nurses with less than five years' experience should limit their résumé to one page. A clear, concise format is extremely important as the résumé is intended to show your professional biography "at a glance." The sample résumés provided in Figures 7–6, 7–7 illustrate the principles of effective résumé writing.

RÉSUMÉ

Patrick Ryan
72 Harding Avenue
New York, New York 11372
(212) 651-7082

Registration:	State boards to be taken July 1983	
Education:	B.S.N. New York University	June 1983
	B.S. New York University	1981
	Major: Chemistry	
Honors:	Pendleton Award for Academic Excellence	1982
	New York State Regents Scholarship	1977–81
Experience:	Bellevue Hospital, Psychiatric Unit Placement: September–December 1982	
	University Hospital Alcoholic Rehabilitation Unit Placement: January–June 1983	
	Kings County Mental Health Center volunteer, 1981–83	
Clinical Areas of Interest:	Psychiatric nursing; neurology	
Organizations:	New York State Student Nurses Association, 1980–83	

References:

Carol Davidson, R.N.	Michael Talbot, M.D.
Nursing Supervisor	Director
Bellevue Hospital	Alcohol Rehabilitation Unit
Psychiatric Unit	University Hospital
New York, NY 11367	New York, NY 11367
Frances Addams	Rev. Karl Matthews
Associate Professor	All Saints Church
New York University	244 East 34 Street
Nursing School	New York, NY 11372
New York, NY 11367	

Figure 7-6. The résumé of a newly graduated nurse.

RÉSUMÉ

Margaret Steiner
201 Beech Street
Morgantown, West Virginia 26505
(304) 293-3107

Registration:	R26032 West Virginia R040032 Maryland	
Education:	B.S.N. West Virginia University	1979
	Certificate in Gerontology West Virginia University	1979
	Diploma—Eastern Shore Hospital School of Nursing	1974
Honors:	American Association of University Women Scholarship	1978
	Edna Davis Award for Excellence, Eastern Shore Hospital School of Nursing	1974
Experience:	Mountain State Nursing Home Morgantown, West Virginia 1980–present Nursing supervisor	
	I am responsible for all nursing care at the home, reporting directly to the administrator.	
	Taylor Nursing Home Osage, West Virginia 1977–1979 Staff nurse	
	I was the R.N. completely responsible for 3–11 care. I supervised the aides and other person- nel involved in patient care.	
	City Hospital Baltimore, Maryland 1974–1977 Staff nurse	

Figure 7-7. The résumé of a nurse with several years' experience.

1974–Staff nurse	Although I did basic medical/surgical nursing, I worked exclusively on the hospital's geriatric unit for two years.
Clinical Areas of Interest:	Geriatric nursing; home health care
Professional Organizations:	ANA West Virginia Nurses Association, District 4
Civic Organizations:	Red Cross Senior Citizens' Council Board of Directors, Monongalia Arts Center
Conferences Attended:	"A Symposium on Alzheimer's Disease," Washington, DC, April 10, 1983 "Psychological Effects of Aging," New York City, November 17, 1983 "Fantasy Therapy for the Geriatric Patient," Cleveland, OH, March 2, 1981 "The Nurse and the Dying Patient," Philadelphia, PA, October 9, 1981 "The Challenge of Geriatric Nursing," New York City, February 2, 1979 "The Aged Person and the Nursing Process," Principal Speaker: Ann Gera Yurick, Pittsburgh, PA, September 26, 1979
Workshops Given:	"Principles of Client/Nurse Interaction for Geriatric Nursing," Morgantown, WV, January 10, 1983 Nursing Implications of Cognitive Regression in the Elderly," Morgantown, WV, August 11, 1983 "Fundamentals of Geriatric Nursing" (This is an in-service workshop for nursing aides which I conduct bi-monthly for Mountain State Nursing Home.)

Figure 7–7. (Continued)

| Paper Delivered: | "Medical Needs of the Senior Citizen," delivered at a meeting of the Monangalia County Health Association, October 24, 1982 |
| References: | Credentials are available from: The Professional Credentials and Personnel Service American Nurses' Association 2420 Pershing Road Kansas City, Missouri   64108 |

Figure 7-7. (Continued)

THE MEMO

In addition to the basic business letter, there is another common type of correspondence among professionals: the memo. This is, in effect, an *internal* business letter, for it is a written communication among members of an agency or unit within an agency. Once you understand the principles behind the use of the memo it's an easy form to write effectively.

The Use of the Memo
The memo is used for all communication that you do not want to leave in verbal form, such as:

- Changes in policy or procedures
- Temporary alterations or building restrictions
- Date, time, and place of meetings
- Introduction of new personnel
- New regulations or changes in existing regulations
- Schedules for either use of equipment or availability of personnel

While most often memos are written *from* those in authority, other personnel may use the form as well, as we illustrated in Chapter 1.

The Purpose of the Memo
The purpose of the memo is to *inform* and to do so quickly and directly. Since this letter is for internal distribution there is no need

for headings with addresses or greetings. In the memo, the writer and audience are probably more closely related than in any other type of writing, and the subject under consideration is something they all have in common. There is no need for any type of introduction to catch the reader's attention.

Form

Although many agencies have a printed memo form, such forms rarely differ in any basic way. There are typically four items in the heading of every memo:

> *To:*
> *From:*
> *Date:*
> *Subject:*

This tells the reader all the essential information. The body or message is similarly concise and succinct. It is also *complete.* If you announce:

> The geriatric in-service meeting will be on January 4, 1983 in Room 406

don't forget to add "at 10:00 A.M." It is vital that all relevant details be included. Sample memos are illustrated in Figures 7-8.

County Hospital

TO: All R.N.s
FROM: Jean Mossberg
               Director of Educational Services
DATE: February 17, 1983
SUBJECT: Workshop: "Care of the Terminally Ill"

The hospital, in cooperation with Fairview Hospice and State College, is sponsoring the workshop "Care of the Terminally Ill" at the Ramada Inn in Fairview on Saturday, February 12, 1983. This workshop is recommended for all R.N.s and required for those enrolled in the hospice certificate program.

Figure 7-8. Sample memo.

Community Mental Health Center

TO: All personnel
FROM: Cynthia Stephenson, Administrative Assistant
DATE: December 9, 1983
SUBJECT: Parking

     Parking decals for next year are now available from the Cashier for $48. A list of regulations is posted on the staff bulletin board and will also be distributed with each decal. Staff are urged to familiarize themselves with these regulations. Drivers who violate these rules risk having their cars towed.

St. Francis Hospital

TO: All personnel
FROM: Michael Callahan, Chairman of the Hospital
               Board
DATE: July 29, 1983
SUBJECT: New Administrator

     Peter Neumann has resigned his position as hospital administrator effective July, 1983. The hospital has appointed a search committee for a new administrator and plans to make an appointment no later than September 31, 1983. In the interim, Paul Reynolds will serve as acting administrator.

Figure 7–8. (continued)

WRITING FOR PUBLICATION

More and more nurses are becoming involved in publishing journal articles and writing books. In nursing, publication is not only for those involved in academia, but nurses in clinical work, home health care, nurse practitioners, and others all frequently share their experiences and expertise with colleagues through publication. Journals like *Nursing '83* and *RN*, which are specifically directed to practicing nurses, get valuable input from professional nurses who are directly involved in client care. Many journals are also directed to aspects of nursing education, research, and administration and solicit manuscripts from nurses involved in those areas of the profession.

Although most undergraduate nursing students may not aspire to publication, writing for publication has definitely become a professional activity for which they should be prepared. At one time research methodology was strictly the province of the master's level. Now it is regularly taught as a component in most B.S.N. programs. In the same way, all professional nurses should be educated in the essentials of writing for publication.

Writing for publication is not as awesome as it may seem, but it should not be taken lightly either. Writing for publication means writing well. The nurse who uses this text profitably and learns to write "with skill and care" has a valuable head start in learning to write for publication. Clear, coherent, precise prose is a transferable art. Write well in your professional responsibilities, and you should be able to write well for publication. As one experienced editor remarked:

> One might wonder why [they] set off 'writing for publication' as though it were a skill separate from writing in general. A command of basic English usage, spelling, composition, and content organization is necessary if a person is to communicate any ideas clearly and comprehensibly, and this holds true for any kind of writing—term paper, research report or journal article. (Lewis, 1980)

The student nurse who writes well in preparing class papers and reports, can learn to write journal articles too. One word of caution, however. Every editor has had the experience of receiving a manuscript with the instructor's "A" marked clearly on the cover. An essay prepared for a class will most likely *not* be immediately publishable in a journal because of the differences in purpose and audience. And in spite of the "A," it may not be written well enough for publication either. Very often in nursing classes, whether they be in baccalaureate, master's, or doctoral programs, the professors are not *primarily* concerned with writing fluency. Often the "paper" is designed as an educative tool, and although writing proficiency is desirable and very much encouraged, an excellent grade on the paper does not mean it is immediately publishable—though it may be *potentially* publishable. (While it is not uncommon to try to publish an essay written for another audience, all subsequent comments deal with the more usual situation of preparing an essay for publication from an original idea.)

In writing for publication a good place to begin is with the basic aspects of our writer's triangle (Fig. 7-9).

Have a Subject

This might also be phrased as "have a purpose." Why are you interested in writing an article? The answer to this question will depend on the nurse's education, experience, and current interests. A professional nurse who regularly reads journals related to his or her practice will undoubtedly feel impelled by a subject at some time. Do you want to:

- **Describe** a method of care you have found helpful in your practice?

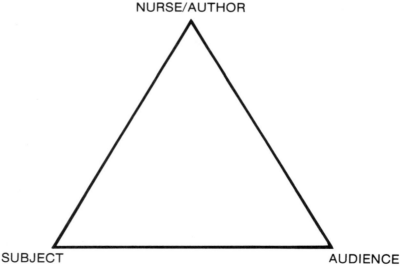

Figure 7-9. The dynamics of the writing process are the same in writing for publication.

- **Narrate** an event related to client care that other nurses will find informative?
- **Explain** how you, or your team, solved a problem related to client care?
- **Report** findings of a research project you conducted?
- **Develop** a theoretical construct related to nursing practice, education, or administration?
- **Take a stand** on an issue in contemporary nursing practice?
- **Offer an opinion** about current practices, standards, or developments in nursing?

All these are suitable purposes for writing a journal article. If you are a professionally educated practicing nurse, it would be unusual for you NOT to have something to say! If you do not see yourself as an author, that may be simply because you haven't yet published, but that doesn't mean you won't be able to write a publishable article. Professional journal articles, regardless of the field, are not written by professional writers, but by professionals in those fields who are active and interested in their profession—whether it be law, sociology, medicine, literature . . . or nursing.

Select an Audience

Any survey of nursing journals will show that there are periodicals devoted to all phases of nursing education, practice, and administration. A nurse who has a subject will rarely be at a loss for an audience. However, the nurse should select his or her audience as soon as possible. It is not uncommon to write (or rewrite) an essay for a particular journal, and your manuscript stands a much better chance of acceptance if it is especially tailored to the requirements of the journal to which it is submitted.

Granted, you may think of yourself as writing for the entire profession, but in fact your essay will probably be directly relevant to two or three journals at most. At this stage of the process of writing for publication, it is important to be informed about nursing periodicals. Some resources are listed at the end of this chapter, but an extremely valuable one deserves mention here. In the June, 1982 issue of *Image*, there is an important article on "Publishing Opportunities for Nurses; A Comparison of 100 Journals," written by

Joann McCloskey and Elizabeth Swanson. The authors' tables show at a glance the number of submissions received by various journals compared with the number accepted for publication, the percentage of unsolicited manuscripts that the journal publishes, and other facts vital for a prospective author to keep in mind. It is helpful to know, for example, that while *AJN* published only 10 percent of the unsolicited manuscripts received in 1980, there are journals that published 60 to 70 percent of the manuscripts they received that same year. Some journals *rarely* publish unsolicited manuscripts. A writer who becomes informed about such details of periodical publication may be able to enhance the possibility of his or her manuscript's receiving an acceptance by choosing the "audience" carefully.

When you decide on a possible "audience" for your essay, if you are not already a regular reader of that particular journal, spend some time going over several issues to confirm that your topic is appropriate for the journal and that the journal has not recently published a similar article to the one you propose to write. In addition, observe the style of writing in that journal. If you note a direct, simple approach, don't develop your own essay informally with a lot of "chatty" comments to the reader. Write in a style appropriate to your topic *and* your prospective audience. Just as if you were presenting a lecture you would adapt both your material and your delivery depending on whether your audience consisted of colleagues, members of a national professional group, clients, or families of clients, you should similarly write with your audience in mind. Your audience is the readers of the publication you have selected.

Queries and Guidelines

Once you have a journal in mind for your prospective article, you might write a "query letter" to inquire if the editor would be interested in receiving your proposed manuscript. Be sure to include a tentative title, the thesis or controlling idea, probable length, and format (any tables, illustrations, etc. that might be required). Some, not all, journals respond to a query. Remember that if you receive a positive response to your inquiry, this is only an agreement to consider your manuscript—not a commitment to publish it. The advantage of the query is to confirm that there is indeed a potential audience for your work. For it might happen that when you write to journal "X" with your idea for an article, they may respond that they would never consider that topic or that they are about to publish a similar article in the next issue! Though you can check to make sure that they have not recently published a similar article, you have no way of knowing how many "accepted" manuscripts are awaiting publication.

Some journals will also send prospective authors guidelines to help in the preparation of the manuscript. This saves you much time in revision as you know the preferred length, style for documentation, and other details of preparation before you begin writing your own manuscript. It may be necessary to write to two or three journals before you are satisfied that you've selected the best audience for your essay. Don't worry that you've narrowed your audience to only one journal. You can only submit your manuscript to one journal at a time, anyway, since simultaneous submissions are considered a breech of professional etiquette and are frowned upon. So it is best to inform yourself about nursing periodicals in general and then try to focus your essay on one particular journal as you prepare your manuscript.

Preparing the Manuscript

Having firmly established *purpose* and *audience*, you are ready to develop and implement your *plan*. You should by now definitely have a goal and controlling idea for your essay; the next step is to formulate a plan, if you have not already done so, either by generating topic sentences or by the more formal topic outline. Everything the writer needs to know about planning is included in Chapter 3.

Once you are satisfied that the plan is appropriate to the topic and the approach to the topic is clear and logical, you are ready to develop your plan by writing the *first draft* of your proposed article. Remember that while you may be used to doing two or three drafts of reports or professional correspondence, the necessity for expressing your thought to a general audience as clearly and coherently as possible may require more revision than you are accustomed to. Don't be discouraged. Even the most experienced writers spend much time in revision. Practice may not make "perfect." but practice helps make "publishable." While you are at this stage of development, there are some important reminders to take note of:

- Don't try to sound "smart." Some writers are so intimidated by the thought of writing for publication that they destroy their writing style with "big" words and convoluted sentence structure. Remember that writing for publication is simply writing well—directly, clearly, accurately.
- Keep your style and tone consistent with your overall topic and with that of the journal for which you're preparing your manuscript.
- When dealing with facts, use recognized and standard authoritative sources, and use the primary sources wherever necessary. For example, if you're discussing Abraham Maslow's hierarchy of needs, refer directly to Maslow, not to the explanation of Maslow's theories in a nursing textbook.

While you're preparing your manuscript it's helpful to get some intelligent feedback from an informed audience, so you should consider asking several of your colleagues to read your work and respond. Most professionals are more than willing to consult in this way, and such responses are always useful because you get an informed but objective view of your presentation.

When you're ready to prepare the final copy of your manuscript for submission, be sure to use good quality paper (16 to 20 lb) and a clean, clear typewriter. Do not use erasable paper as it smudges the copy in handling. Many journals require more than one copy of the manuscript, and you should also always keep a copy for yourself. You will probably want to have Xerox copies made as carbons are more difficult to type and also are easily smudged.

Type your essay double-spaced with wide margins (about 1½ inches). If your manuscript is accepted, it will be copy edited and the wide margins are helpful to the copy editor. Type your name and address in the upper left hand corner of the first page; number subsequent pages, prefacing the number with your last name. Do not use a cover sheet or any type of folder. If you cannot prepare a clear, clean copy without noticeable erasures and strikeovers, it is worthwhile to pay a manuscript typist.

Prepare a cover letter for your submission. Address the letter to the editor (you can find his or her name by looking at any issue of the journal) or to the person who responded to your query letter if you received a response. Inform him or her that you are submitting your manuscript for consideration. If you have had previous correspondence, refer to that. If this is your first contact with the journal you may give some brief, appropriate information about yourself or your essay. The fact that you have ten years' experience working with the mentally retarded may be relevant if that is the topic of your essay, or you may want to mention that you are an R.N. who was formerly an L.P.N. and now has a B.S.N. if your essay is on changes in education for nurses. The cover letter should be fairly brief (certainly never longer than a page) and to the point:

"I hope you will consider my essay suitable for publication in (name of journal)."

Note: Since an "article" is the *published* form, refer to your submission as your manuscript or essay.

Submitting Your Essay
Send your manuscript and cover letter to the attention of the person to whom the cover letter is addressed. Mail your submission flat, in a manila envelope. Be sure to include a *stamped, self-addressed, return envelope* so that your manuscript can be returned to you at no cost to the journal. This is a professional courtesy. Don't think of this as anticipating rejection; most *accepted* essays are returned with copy editor's corrections for your approval.

Waiting
This is probably the most difficult part of the entire process of "writing for publication." Once you've placed your "child" in the mail, you must await the results of the review process, hoping the reviewers will look kindly on your offspring. When your manuscript is received by a journal, it is subject to either of two types of review process. An *internal review* means that it is evaluated by several members of the editorial board of the journal itself. A *refereed*

review indicates that the editor sends copies of the manuscript to qualified and experienced professionals for evaluation. In either case, your work is given close and serious scrutiny and evaluated according to well-established criteria. A reader cannot recommend either publication or rejection of a manuscript without detailing reasons for that opinion. This process of review usually takes several months. Some journals acknowledge receipt of your manuscript at once and estimate the length of review time needed. With other journals you may hear nothing at all until the review process is completed. It is acceptable to inquire about the status of your manuscript, but you should wait at least six months before inquiring. By that time the journal should have responded to you in some way, so it is wise to inquire. Manuscripts *do* get lost in the mail, unfortunately. You may have to wait even longer for a decision, but your letter of inquiry may spur an editor to contact a reader who may be taking too much time with your essay.

The Response

What happens if despite all your preparation and care, your manuscript is rejected? Don't despair. Though "despair" may seem like a strong word, it's extremely disheartening to get back a "rejected" manuscript on which you've spent a great deal of time and effort. Keep in mind that in journal publishing (and academic publishing in general) many manuscripts with merit are rejected because of publication restrictions, such as problems of space ("We receive 600 manuscripts a year and can only publish 60"), appeal ("We have two articles in press right now on treating the depressive client, and we can't consider another for at least three years"), and other editorial concerns that you may not be able to anticipate. Unless you receive negative comments about your presentation, it is appropriate (and wise) to submit your essay to another suitable journal.

If the editor and/or the readers have made comments critical of your presentation, these reviews should help you strengthen your essay for future submission. Sometimes an editor will invite resubmission in a letter of rejection; sometimes he or she will suggest another journal for which your essay seems more appropriate. Remember that when you are writing for publication, no comments about your work are intended (or should be taken) personally. A response to your essay, regardless how negative, should be helpful in improving it. Unfortunately, some journals have been known to send merely a form rejection that says nothing specific about the manuscript. In such cases, it is acceptable to write and ask for the readers' reviews.

If the journal *accepts* your manuscript for publication, there will certainly be at least a brief period of euphoria. Then you must get down to the business of seeing your manuscript to print. Even with an accepted manuscript, you may receive suggestions for revision, or you may simply receive the copy-edited manuscript for review and return. In any case, the publication process is expensive, and deadlines are important. You must make every effort to meet whatever dates are given you by the editor. Some journals also send you galley proofs later on for correction; others don't. In the event you receive proofs, remember that changes at this stage of the publication process are extremely costly, and you are only expected to check for any errors which may have slipped by. You are *not* to make any extensive revisions at this point. Most publishers charge for changes made in galley.

Journals almost always have a backlog of accepted articles, so it may be from six months to two years more before you "appear." Eventually, however, you will receive a copy of the journal containing your article, and you can enjoy your new status as an "author." Like all other professional accomplishments, you've earned it.

WRITING A BOOK

There is an increasing demand for quality books in nursing education and practice, and professional nurses are writing them. There are two basic ways that you may become involved in writing a book. You may be employed in some area of nursing practice or education and become aware of a need for a book for some particular aspect of your work and may contact a publisher about the possibility of writing one to supply this need. Similarly, you may become known for your work in a particular area, and the publisher may contact you about a perceived need for a publication in that area.

Don't be misled into thinking that writing a book is exactly the same as writing an article—only longer. Of course, the writing process remains the same regardless of the task, but the scope of a book makes the preparation and planning much more detailed, and psychologically writing a book is a much more *consuming* process. While you may already be accustomed to spending several months preparing a journal article, it is possible that the book may take several *years* of your time and energy. If you are writing in addition to working full time as a professional nurse, you must be prepared for the extended commitment that the book involves. In addition, your commitment is not only to yourself. Most nursing books are written "under contract," which means that you have a commitment to the publisher as well and specific deadlines to meet.

Planning

Whether you contact the publisher or are contacted by the publisher, the first step is usually the submission of a prospectus. A prospectus is a detailed plan of your book, chapter by chapter; an explanation of the need for this particular book; a description of the audience to which it will be addressed; an analysis and comparison to other books (if any) on the same topic by other publishers; a presentation of any special features you plan. This prospectus is *usually* 15 to 30 pages, depending on the scope of the book planned. Be as thorough as possible with your prospectus because this (1) establishes your purpose; (2) identifies your audience; and (3) details your plan. The more precise and developed your prospectus, the better your chances of receiving a contract, and the easier the actual writing of the book will be. If you have a good prospectus, writing the book becomes the process of developing this basic plan, and you minimize the unexpected problems that always arise with any extended writing task.

The acquisitions editor (person responsible for "signing" the book and seeing the manuscript to production) may suggest alterations and revisions of the prospectus. Be cooperative. A publisher has a significant investment in the production of a single book and must be certain of the manuscript's content before entering into contract with a writer. If at any time in this process you feel that your concept of the book differs significantly from the concept the publisher has in mind, and you don't seem able to come to an agreement, you should withdraw your prospectus and seek another publisher. Once you sign a contract, you have an obligation to produce the book that the publisher has contracted for. It is no longer solely your own project (as writing an article usually is), but is a cooperative venture between you and the publisher.

The Contract

Once your prospectus is accepted, the acquisitions editor will acquaint you with the responsibilities of the contract, the nature of royalty payment, etc. While the contract is being negotiated, be honest about your ability to meet suggested deadlines. Do not promise a finished manuscript too soon in your enthusiasm for the project; be as realistic as possible about the time it will take. Obviously, in an extended project like a book there may be unexpected delays due to illness or family emergencies, but it is a professional responsibility to keep to deadlines as closely as possible. So estimate the time you will need honestly. Once that date is arrived at, it is a firm commitment to the publisher.

Writing

Once you embark on the actual writing of the manuscript, you will realize that a book is produced in segments, and the individual segments are written much like any other essay you've done. Many publishers have an "Author's Guide" to assist you in the preparation of the manuscript according to their specifications. In addition, your editor will be in regular contact with you, and should you have any difficulties or questions about the manuscript, he or she will be able to advise you. Your responsibility is to prepare your manuscript by faithfully following the plan indicated in the prospectus. In the event some radical changes seem to be indicated, you must discuss them with the editor. You cannot offer the publisher a manuscript that differs significantly from the accepted prospectus.

Production

Once your completed manuscript goes into production, it is usually eight months to a year before the book is finally in print. During that time, you will be contacted several times by the publisher. You may be asked to review the copy-edited manuscript to approve stylistic changes in your writing. You may be asked to review galley proofs for any errors that may have occurred in typesetting the book. When you receive these copies for review, you will be asked to return them by a specific date. Be *absolutely faithful* to these deadlines as the entire production schedule may depend on your reliability at this stage of the project. If you have agreed to provide the book's index, it will be done from page proofs, and the publisher usually cannot give you too much time. If your schedule is very busy at the time when the index comes due you would be well advised to ask for a professional indexer rather than hold up production of the book for your index.

Print

When your book finally "comes out," the publisher usually takes care of advertising and promotion. You can relax and bask in the admiration of relatives, friends, and colleagues. You have completed a valuable professional activity and may find yourself invited to write more articles and other books. Increasingly, the nurse/author is not an anomaly, but a vital and respected member of the profession.

REFERENCE

Lewis EP: As the editor sees it. Nurs Outlook 11:689, 1980.

EXERCISES

I. Prepare your résumé according to the guidelines in this chapter.

II. Read the "positions open" section in several nursing journals and in local newspapers. Select two to three positions for which you are suited and write sample letters of application to develop facility.

III. Write a letter of inquiry to a journal asking for their authors' guidelines. (Do not mail the letter unless you have a serious interest in publishing.)
IV. Write a "letter to the editor" of a nursing journal in response to a recent article.
 V. Read several issues of *AJN* and *Nursing Research*. Write a brief essay in which you compare and contrast the types of articles in the journals and the styles of writing.

ADDITIONAL RESOURCES

Binger J: Writing for publication: A survey of nursing journal editors. J Nurs Admin 9:50-52, 1979.

McCloskey JC, Swanson E: Publishing opportunities for nurses: A Comparison of 100 journals. *Image* 14:50-56, 1982.

O'Connor A: Writing for Nursing Publications. Thorofare, NJ, Charles B. Slack, Inc., 1976.

Schweer KD, Warner SD: An Author's Guide to Journals in Nursing and Related Fields. New York, Haworth Press, 1982.

APPENDIX I

Spelling Demons

This list includes words frequently misspelled by college students. You should try to arrange to be "tested" on this list to assess your own spelling proficiency—or lack thereof. Simply have a spouse or friend read the words to you while you try to *write* them correctly. All of these are common words that every professionally educated adult should be able to spell without consulting a dictionary. Those you misspell, you should make an effort to learn. This is part of the process of learning to write "with skill and care."

abbreviate	apparatus	beneficial	competition
absence	apparently	boundaries	completely
accidentally	appearance	Britain	compulsory
accommodate	appreciate	bureaucracy	concede
accompanying	appropriate	business	conference
accomplish	approximately	calendar	confidentially
accumulate	arctic	candidate	conscience
acknowledge	argument	category	conscientious
acquaintance	arithmetic	cemetery	conscious
acquire	association	certain	consistent
across	athletics	characteristic	continuous
aggravate	attendance	chosen	controversial
always	audience	commission	convenient
amateur	auxiliary	committee	counterfeit
among	awkward	communism	criticism
analysis	barbarous	comparative	criticize
analytical	basically	competent	curiosity

curriculum	forty	obstacle	repetition
decision	frantically	occasionally	respectively
definitely	guarantee	occurrence	restaurant
describe	height	omission	ridiculous
description	humorous	opportunity	sandwich
desperate	hurried	optimist	satisfactorily
dictionary	imagination	original	schedule
difference	immediately	pamphlet	secretary
disappear	incidentally	parallel	separately
disappoint	incredible	particularly	significant
disastrous	independence	pastime	similar
discipline	indispensable	permissible	specifically
dissatisfied	inevitable	perseverance	successful
doesn't	influential	persuade	surprise
efficient	initiative	physically	suspicious
eligible	intelligence	possession	syllable
eliminate	intentionally	practically	synonymous
embarrass	interrupt	preceding	synthetic
eminent	irrelevant	prejudice	temperament
emphasize	irresistible	preparation	thorough
enthusiastic	irritation	prevalent	together
environment	knowledge	privilege	tragedy
equipment	legitimate	probably	truly
especially	liable	procedure	twelfth
exaggerated	livelihood	proceed	unanimous
exceed	loneliness	professional	undoubtedly
exceptionally	maintenance	psychiatrist	unnecessarily
existence	marriage	psychologist	until
experience	miniature	pursue	usually
extraordinary	miscellaneous	quantity	various
extremely	naturally	realize	Wednesday
familiar	necessary	really	whether
fascinate	ninety	recognize	wholly
February	nowadays	recommend	
finally	oblige	remembrance	

APPENDIX II

Completed Exercises

Responses to exercises presented in Chapter 2:

   I. Gerontology is a rapidly expanding speciality among health care and social service professions. Research in the problems of the elderly in society has led to an awareness of the stereotypes with which many Americans approach the aged and a reexamination of our traditional ways of treating older people. Old age, usually considered that period from age 65 on, is a somewhat arbitrary designation depending on an individual's ability to adapt to the inevitable physical loss, a loss which varies from person to person. The contemporary gerontologist must have a knowledge of the physical and psychological needs of the individual and, above all, be a caring professional interested in each client's well-being.

  II.   **1.** The students will be responsible for medications, vital signs, and treatments.
     2. With the advent of the pediatric nurse practitioner, well-child care has undergone some significant changes.
     3. Nurses who work in the Emergency Department are able to handle stressful situations.
     4. Mrs. Lomen, the woman with five children, doesn't want to use birth control.
     5. Mrs. Bailey denies pain, yet she has been crying and is unable to sleep.
     6. Mr. Jones will be discharged in the morning, and his family will be coming for him.

7. There are four steps in the nursing process: assessment, planning, intervention, and evaluation.
8. In reviewing the chart, the supervisor noticed several errors.
9. Brain-stem depression was caused by a tumor.
10. University Hospital offers specialization in Obstetrics, Urology, Neurology, ICU, Pediatrics, and Oncology.
11. She was described by the psychologists as an overly protective mother.
12. Well-child care can be provided by a family nurse practitioner or a pediatric nurse practitioner.
13. Knowing the prognosis was poor, the health care team requested a meeting with the family.
14. Nursing has struggled to attain professional status but is hampered by the entry into practice issue (or "entry into practice" issue).
15. The health history includes demographic data, the past health history, the family history, a review of systems, sociological and psychological data, and information concerning the present state of the client.
16. After the medication was given, the patient's behavior became extremely agitated.
17. Nursing, like any other profession, requires dedication and commitment.
18. The World Health Organization defines health as a state of complete physical, mental, and social well-being—not merely the absence of disease.
19. The Primary Care Clinic, which is run by nurses, is located on East Main.
20. In my opinion, nurses who work in primary care settings need physical assessment skills.
21. The following areas will be covered in this course: interviewing skills, data collection, techniques used in physical assessment, and proper documentation of findings.
22. An adequate diet includes the proper balance of carbohydrates, protein and fat.
23. Because it was the students' first day on the unit, the instructor remained close at hand.

24. Mr. Morrison, who was admitted for gall bladder surgery, has developed chest pain.

25. The students have performed the tasks in the skills lab, but they still require supervision on the nursing unit.

26. Procedures which require invasive techniques are harder to perform.

27. Sensing the tension on the staff, the head nurse called a meeting.

28. A thorough assessment includes the physical, psychological, and psychosocial aspects of the client.

29. After assessing the client's health status, the nurse documented her findings.

30. Language, poverty, and cultural beliefs can be barriers to health care delivery for ethnic people.

Index